PRAISE FOR *REINVENT*

"*Reinvent* captures the critical contribution of attitude, behaviors, and culture to developing a compelling vision, comprehensive strategy and plan, and relentless implementation process. Thank you, Fred, for helping leaders become their best!"

—*Alan Mulally, President and CEO, The Ford Motor Company*

"Fred is one of the outstanding transformational leaders of all time in the pharmaceutical industry. He proved, several times, that against all odds, he had the formula for success and shareholders benefitted handsomely. Everyone loved being on his team. He encourages people to think outside their normal patterns and challenges them to achieve greatness. He congregates talented people around a well-thought-out business mission and then empowers them to act without fear of failure. *Reinvent* is a must-read for any executive who aspires to run a company."

—*Thomas J. Neff, Chairman of Spencer Stuart, U.S.*

"I have had the honor of working with many of the world's greatest leaders. I rank Fred Hassan as one of the top five. Fred has helped more organizations reinvent themselves than anyone I have met! *Reinvent* is Fred's gift to you! Please apply what you learn in this book to reinvent your own life and the lives of the people around you."

—*Marshall Goldsmith, recognized among world's top 50 influential leadership thinkers* (Harvard Business Review)

"Fred Hassan shares his practical playbook for change leadership by demonstrating how attitude, behavior and culture can lead to transformation, excellence in execution and sustained high performance. The book is full of good common sense and real world examples of leadership."

—*Alex Gorsky, Chairman and CEO, Johnson & Johnson*

"Company success depends on strong leadership. Fred's recipe for success: select top talent, help them develop expertise, lead by example."

—*P. Roy Vagelos, M.D., Retired Chairman and CEO, Merck & Co., Inc.*

"Fred Hassan blends his triumphant first-hand experience with the wisdom of a first-class mind to share an engaging, accessible, manual of essential leadership lessons. Having seen peer CEOs hang on his every word in private top leadership forums for many years, I have begged Fred Hassan to go public with this compelling gift of knowledge for a long time. I will certainly be using it at our top executive forums and leadership programs on campus!"

—*Professor Jeffrey Sonnenfeld, Senior Associate Dean,*
Yale School of Management

"Fred Hassan passes on his vast and winning know-how that will help you power up your people to drive breakthrough results. He's done it and so can you. There's nothing like learning from the master."

—*David Novak, Chairman and CEO, Yum! Brands, Inc.*

"In *Reinvent*, Fred Hassan shares a winning philosophy that builds on the crucial role of people to power up an organization's potential. Hassan delivers a proven actionable change leadership playbook to evolve and reinvent leadership effectiveness supported by evidence from his exceptional track record as an effective and value-creating CEO, with an exceptional reputation from his peers and shareholders alike."

—*Andrew N. Liveris, Chairman and CEO,*
The Dow Chemical Company

reinvent

reinvent

A LEADER'S PLAYBOOK
FOR SERIAL SUCCESS

FRED HASSAN

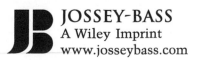

JOSSEY-BASS
A Wiley Imprint
www.josseybass.com

Published by Jossey-Bass
A Wiley Imprint
Published simultaneously in the United States of America and Canada.
www.josseybass.com

Jossey-Bass books and products are available through most bookstores. To contact
Jossey-Bass directly, call our Customer Care Department within the US at 800-956-7739,
outside the U.S. at 317-572-3986, or fax 317-572-4002.

Wiley publishes in a variety of print and electronic formats and by print-on-demand.
Some material included with standard print versions of this book may not be included
in e-books or in print-on-demand. If this book refers to media such as a CD or DVD
that is not included in the version you purchased, you may download this material
at http://booksupport.wiley.com. For more information about Wiley products, visit
www.wiley.com.

ISBN 978-1-118-52985-0 (print); 978–1–118–52988–1 (ebk);
978–1–118–52989–8 (ebk); 978–1–118–52986–7 (ebk)

Production Credits
Managing Editor: Alison Maclean
Executive Editor: Don Loney
Production Editor: Pauline Ricablanca
Cover Design: Adrian So
Cover Photography: © FreeSoulProduction / iStockphoto
Author Photograph: Valerie Noell
Composition: Thomson Digital
Printer: Courier

Printed in the United States of America

1 2 3 4 5 CR 17 16 15 14 13

To my wife Noreen
and the thousands of colleagues who committed to winning
as a team. Their inspiration made this Playbook possible.

Contents

List of Figures

Foreword

Skeptics often speculate that a successful chief executive officer's performance may be due to tailwinds—or to chance. But even skeptics would agree that if there is a pattern of success—repeated serially—then *that* CEO *is* making the difference. Fred Hassan is one of *those* CEOs.

Frequently described as a "serial turnaround expert," Fred is a fixer of companies in distress. At company after company that has found itself in desperate straits, he has been called in to stop the bleeding. What is less well known is that he is also a transformation leader. He has transformed companies and created unexpected, long-term shareholder values. This is why, in July of 2009, the TV personality Jim Cramer said, "The first person I would nominate to put on a wall of fame would be Fred Hassan."

How has Fred done it? Like other serially successful CEOs, Fred has a *Playbook* that he uses again and again. He relies heavily on what he calls the *ABC Advantage*. He believes that attitude drives behavior; behavior drives culture; and culture then fosters executional excellence and sustainable high performance. According to Fred, *attitude*, *behavior* and *culture* (ABC) are productivity advantages, in addition to business acumen and drive. In this way, he creates company cultures that develop effective strategies and powerful execution.

Fred builds teams who punch above their weight. Fred encourages his people first to build strength on the inside, then to leverage that strength on the outside. At every step in his career, Fred has been a visible leader, leading from the front. Even as a top executive, he is on the factory floor, with customers and in the research labs—listening, learning and inspiring. He asks probing questions and demonstrates that he understands the challenges of his front-line colleagues. Fred emphasizes that "we are one company, one culture, one team, because of the attitude and behaviors we bring to our work." This is his rallying cry.

Many of the crucial behaviors he encourages have a decidedly yin and yang ring to them, like healthy anxiety, contagious energy, realistic optimism, constructive impatience and confident humility—which leads me to another trait. Not only is he a skilled leader at fixing, building and maximizing, but he is also a person of integrity. During the 2002–3 time period when Fred was chairman of the pharmaceutical trade association, the CEOs agreed to voluntary guidelines on ethical promotion and clinical trials. After years of deliberation by the board, this action was made possible because Fred and his colleagues believed in a new and transparent way of operating to benefit the patient.

His personal role modeling and humanity have yielded a large corps of people who are grateful to have been with him. While Fred has been consistently successful in turning businesses around, he has also succeeded in developing generations of future CEOs. Brent Saunders, who is now the CEO of Bausch + Lomb, is one such noteworthy example. Attitude, behavior and culture develop talent for the future.

Since the mid-1990s, I have known Fred and observed him at CEO gatherings, such as The Business Council, and kept abreast of his efforts at the various companies he has led. I knew after meeting him for the first time that he would be a CEO to watch and to learn from.

Before chairing Bausch + Lomb in March of 2010, Fred's most profound success story as CEO began in 2003 when he was recruited after the Pfizer/Pharmacia merger to become chairman and CEO of Schering-Plough. This pharmaceutical giant could hardly have been in worse shape. Its revenues were plunging; it had no promising products ready to pick up the slack; and various authorities of the U.S. government had launched investigations with no end in sight. *Fortune* magazine predicted that "Fred Hassan may be heading toward his first high-profile failure," and that it would be "miraculous" if the company survived.

Fred saw something else. He got going with his Playbook— engaging the customers, the investors, the Schering-Plough people and, especially, the company's frontline managers. He knew from experience that enlisting the passionate commitment of the employees was the key to the company's return to health, and he assured them that they were valued, saying, "If we stay focused, have faith in ourselves and do the right things, we will come out of the darkness."

His approach worked. After fixing what was broken, Schering-Plough embarked on 17 straight quarters of double-digit revenue growth. What was a cash burn of almost a billion dollars a year turned into a positive cash flow of $2 billion. Fred also brought the company's troubles with agencies of the U.S. government under control. But even more importantly, the company built trust for the future by making authentic remedial changes to its culture and its processes. During Fred's tenure of six and a half years, Schering-Plough's stock rose 62 percent, versus a drop of 21 percent for the unweighted basket of six peers.[1]

---

[1] SGP proxy statement peers over the period 4/25/03 to 11/3/09 (Abbot, Bristol-Myers Squibb, Johnson & Johnson, Eli Lilly and Company, Merck & Co., Pfizer). All numbers are operating (i.e., non-GAAP) numbers.

No one should have been surprised at the turnaround. Prior to taking charge at Schering-Plough, Fred had already worked his magic at several other companies. I saw firsthand how Fred saved the failing merger of Sweden's Pharmacia and Michigan's Upjohn (PNU) in 1997 to 1998. The PNU turnaround was so powerful that by the time it was actually declared a turnaround in October 1998, the stock had already risen 50 percent during the previous 12 months. Only two years after taking charge at PNU, Fred was already on *Worth*'s 50 Best CEOs list (May 1999). Ten years and two companies later, Fred was still doing well. *Institutional Investor* picked him from among his peers for the America's Best CEOs 2008 list.

Fred's extraordinary career began with an extraordinary background. Born in 1945 in Pakistan, "Farid" became better known as Fred to his siblings and his classmate friends. His father, Fida Hassan, a civil servant and statesman, had a long and successful career that ultimately ended in 1977 when he had a fatal heart attack in his New Delhi office while serving as Pakistan's ambassador to India. Fred's mother, Zeenat Hassan, was a women's rights advocate. Her group's famous "March to the President's House" in 1960 was part of a movement to enact new laws to protect women and children.

Fred grew up in Pakistan, then obtained his degree in chemical engineering from the Imperial College of Science, Technology and Medicine in London. In 1967, he returned to Pakistan where he worked in fertilizer sales and marketing. In 1969, he showed how smart he was in marrying Noreen, and, a year later, they decided to immigrate to the United States, where Fred obtained an MBA from Harvard. While at Harvard, Fred was hired by the pharmaceutical giant Sandoz (now Novartis), and spent the next 17 years getting one challenging assignment after another, demonstrating success and getting promoted. Only 11 years out of Harvard, he was asked to turn around the company's largest operating unit, Sandoz US. He then continued to show serial success at four large global companies—Wyeth, PNU, Pharmacia and Schering-Plough.

Fred is still running hard. For him, reinvention is its own intrinsic reward. His leadership and management expertise have become valued well beyond the pharmaceutical industry. The renowned private equity firm Warburg Pincus invited him to be a partner and managing director, and to help across its broad port-folio of companies. He is currently chairman of Bausch + Lomb, a board member of the media and entertainment giant Time Warner and, on January 1, 2013, also became Chairman of Avon as an independent director.

Like me, readers will see the keys to serial success through Fred's experience and his Playbook. There are few better to learn from.

Dr. Ram Charan
Bestselling author and business adviser

Author's Note

This book is my Playbook, and it contains my philosophy, strategies and practices that have proven successful throughout my career. It describes how I have been able to salvage almost impossible situations, and transform entire operations and companies. I give credit to my colleagues, who made extraordinary things happen. It was always, *always* a team effort.

Reinvent illustrates my practical leadership approaches with observations, learnings and anecdotes from different times in my life. Since I don't discuss these life-shaping experiences in chronological order, I have included, for easy reference, a timeline at the end of this section. Like other CEOs, I have made my share of mistakes, and have had my share of embarrassments. I learned as much as I could from them and kept moving forward. In fact, this Playbook places a high degree of importance on learning from mistakes.

Since beginning my business career in fertilizer sales in Pakistan in 1967 with an affiliate of Hercules,[1] I have worked for large, complex, innovation-driven companies—Sandoz, Wyeth,[2] Pharmacia & Upjohn, Pharmacia and Schering-Plough. In the interest of brevity and clarity, I will often refer to these companies by their stock symbols. Many of the companies in this changing and consolidating industry have been subsumed into new corporate names and stock symbols, either by mega-mergers or through name changes. Sandoz, for example, became Novartis (NVS) after Sandoz merged with Ciba-Geigy in 1996. Pharmacia & Upjohn (PNU) joined with Monsanto (MTC) to become a new combined company called Pharmacia (PHA) in 2000. PHA subsequently spun off its agricultural subsidiary as "new" Monsanto (MON) in June 2002. PHA subsequently merged with Pfizer (PFE) in April 2003, as did Schering-Plough (SGP) with Merck (MRK) in November 2009. Wyeth (WYE) merged with PFE in 2009, 12 years after I left.

I believe that successful leadership is more an attitude than a system. In these pages I describe a number of traits that, as Ram points out in the Foreword of this book, move from attitude to results. The advantage discussed in this book applies also to situations with different scales and complexities than the global corporations mentioned in the previous paragraph. Whether the aspirant is today's or tomorrow's CEO, or an executive in any organization, big or small, this Playbook will help as long as he or she is committed to developing and sustaining a leader's attitude.

---

[1] A global chemical company headquartered in Wilmington, Delaware.

[2] As pharmaceuticals became more important in the original American Home Products Corporation, the corporate entity name merged with its pharmaceutical name, Wyeth, in 2002.

Not only will readers and their teams and organizations be more effective if they follow this Playbook, they will also be more satisfied and fulfilled, and will have more fun. I believe that positive attitudes lead to productive behaviors, which in turn build stronger cultures. Cultures continue to strengthen not only because operational or financial goals are met, but also because of the personal satisfaction people feel when they contribute to a winning effort. I believe personal satisfaction reinforces attitudes, which then keeps the wheel in motion.

I have spent most of my career in Big Pharma, but I also draw upon my learnings from other industries. I have been—and still am—engaged with other industries through my operational experiences (for example, chemicals, consumer, agriculture, devices, foods, diagnostics, services), my board work, my participation in cross-industry groups (such as the G100 group of CEOs) and my partner work with a multi-industry private equity firm. I can, therefore, say with great confidence that my observations apply across industries. Although the Schering-Plough example is often mentioned in this book, since it was my most recent experience as a CEO, I used the strategies and concepts outlined in this Playbook in the other operations I led. Only the descriptors may have been different. In discussing my CEO experiences, however, I don't pretend to have expertise in all business, medical or legal matters.

Why the "Reinvent" title? The people I have seen as good leaders are the ones who *always* want to get better. Their attitude includes being restless with the status quo. This title is not just about personal reinvention, it is also about change leadership and influencing others to get better (in other words, reinventing one's environment).

A couple of editorial notes: The opinions mentioned here are my own and do not reflect those of my past or present affiliations. The quoted comments are based on my remembrances and may differ from the recollections of others. Also, some names have been omitted because of my confidentiality obligations, or to respect sensitivities.

Some chapters and sections are longer than others. Length should not lead to an assumption of significance. What is important is to understand that all points in this Playbook come together as a whole.

You will observe that I vary usage of pronoun and tense, as events shift between the past and present. I often address the reader in direct language (i.e., "you" and "we"). All these are done to facilitate the practical leadership learnings in this book.

The financial figures mentioned in this book are operational numbers (i.e., non-GAAP[3]). These numbers, which are customarily used by financial analysts, exclude certain accounting conventions and special items in order to have better clarity and comparability to the real operating situation.

Finally, my motive for writing *Reinvent*. I decided to write this book because friends and colleagues were telling me that many of my unusual experiences and learnings could help those who aspire to excel as serially successful leaders. Many young people regularly reach out to me for coaching. It is fulfilling to help others, although I admit I don't have as much time to help them as I would like. I agreed with my peers that this is a good time to share my Playbook, despite the fact that I am still on a learning curve as a partner at a leading private equity firm and as chairman of a large, and now reinvented, global health-care company.

The learning never stops!

---

[3] Generally accepted accounting principles.

Life and Career Timeline

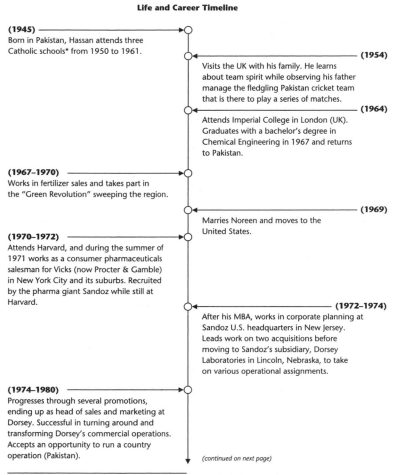

(1945) ————————————————○
Born in Pakistan, Hassan attends three
Catholic schools* from 1950 to 1961.

———————————————— **(1954)**
Visits the UK with his family. He learns
about team spirit while observing his father
manage the fledgling Pakistan cricket team
that is there to play a series of matches.

———————————————— **(1964)**
Attends Imperial College in London (UK).
Graduates with a bachelor's degree in
Chemical Engineering in 1967 and returns
to Pakistan.

(1967–1970) ————————————————○
Works in fertilizer sales and takes part in
the "Green Revolution" sweeping the region.

———————————————— **(1969)**
Marries Noreen and moves to the
United States.

(1970–1972) ————————————————○
Attends Harvard, and during the summer of
1971 works as a consumer pharmaceuticals
salesman for Vicks (now Procter & Gamble)
in New York City and its suburbs. Recruited
by the pharma giant Sandoz while still at
Harvard.

———————————————— **(1972–1974)**
After his MBA, works in corporate planning at
Sandoz U.S. headquarters in New Jersey.
Leads work on two acquisitions before
moving to Sandoz's subsidiary, Dorsey
Laboratories in Lincoln, Nebraska, to take
on various operational assignments.

(1974–1980) ————————————————○
Progresses through several promotions,
ending up as head of sales and marketing at
Dorsey. Successful in turning around and
transforming Dorsey's commercial operations.
Accepts an opportunity to run a country
operation (Pakistan).   *(continued on next page)*

---

*In Lahore: Convent of Jesus and Mary and then St. Anthony High School. In Rawalpindi: St. Mary's Academy.

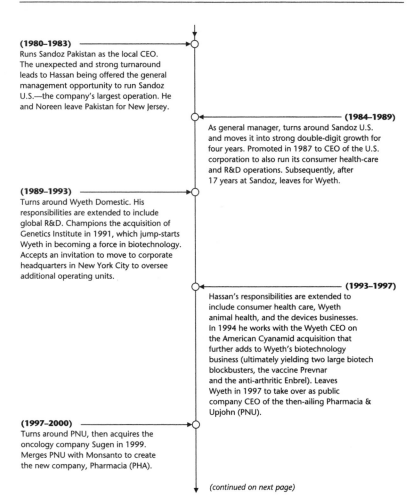

(1980–1983)

Runs Sandoz Pakistan as the local CEO. The unexpected and strong turnaround leads to Hassan being offered the general management opportunity to run Sandoz U.S.—the company's largest operation. He and Noreen leave Pakistan for New Jersey.

(1984–1989)

As general manager, turns around Sandoz U.S. and moves it into strong double-digit growth for four years. Promoted in 1987 to CEO of the U.S. corporation to also run its consumer health-care and R&D operations. Subsequently, after 17 years at Sandoz, leaves for Wyeth.

(1989–1993)

Turns around Wyeth Domestic. His responsibilities are extended to include global R&D. Champions the acquisition of Genetics Institute in 1991, which jump-starts Wyeth in becoming a force in biotechnology. Accepts an invitation to move to corporate headquarters in New York City to oversee additional operating units.

(1993–1997)

Hassan's responsibilities are extended to include consumer health care, Wyeth animal health, and the devices businesses. In 1994 he works with the Wyeth CEO on the American Cyanamid acquisition that further adds to Wyeth's biotechnology business (ultimately yielding two large biotech blockbusters, the vaccine Prevnar and the anti-arthritic Enbrel). Leaves Wyeth in 1997 to take over as public company CEO of the then-ailing Pharmacia & Upjohn (PNU).

(1997–2000)

Turns around PNU, then acquires the oncology company Sugen in 1999. Merges PNU with Monsanto to create the new company, Pharmacia (PHA).

(continued on next page)

(2000–2003)

At PHA, oversees a 19 percent annual compounded growth rate in earnings per share (1999–2002). Monsanto's agricultural business is spun out and later becomes a huge success. Pfizer approaches Pharmacia for a merger and then agrees to a 44 percent premium (trailing 30 days average basis) and the transaction closes in April 2003. Hassan is immediately recruited to become CEO of the then-failing company Schering-Plough (SGP).

(2003–2009)

Leads the turnaround and transformation of SGP. Then acquires Organon Biosciences in 2007. This $16-billion acquisition turns EPS accretive in its first full quarter. Merck approaches SGP for a merger and then agrees to a 44 percent premium (trailing 30 days average basis) and the transaction closes in November 2009.

(2009 to publication)

Joins Warburg Pincus as senior advisor, subsequently accepts invitation to become partner and managing director. Named chairman of Bausch & Lomb, while continuing as board member of Time Warner and director of Avon Products. Named independent (non-executive) chairman of Avon on January 1, 2013.

Introduction

May 31, 2012, St. Regis Hotel, New York City: Onstage with me is Bill Ackman (hedge-fund activist), along with Jack Welch (ex-CEO, General Electric) as the moderator. About a hundred CEOs are intently listening to our discussion on making company managements more accountable. As we intensely debate shareholder activism and corporate governance, I remind the audience that we must also think of the people in organizations who actually make success happen. I can see heads nodding as I speak. *People make the decisive difference.* That is the main subject of this book.

This book is about reinvention and serial success as manifested by repeated and sustained high performance—for the individual, for the team and for the company. It illustrates how what I call the *ABC Advantage* is a common denominator for those who succeed again

FIGURE I.1 The ABC Advantage
Source: SGP/Merck

and again. Having met or observed dozens of CEOs from around the world, and having screened dozens of my CEO peers for the CEO of the Year award as a member of the CEO of the Year Selection Committee for the Chief Executive Group, the ABC Advantage almost always shows up as part of the profile of those CEOs who are serial achievers. The ABC Advantage works because attitude stimulates behavior, behavior drives culture and culture fosters executional excellence, which produces extraordinary and sustained performance. (See Figure I.1: The ABC Advantage.)

While business acumen and drive are critical for leaders, ABC provides the extra advantage that leads to repeated wins.

I believe that in every aspiring and committed individual, in every team and in every company, the potential exists to deliver performance beyond what is commonly viewed as achievable. The ability to power up this potential is what creates extraordinary change, including turnarounds and transformations. It's in our power to do more with what we have. It's in our power to fulfill our own potential. It's not where our aspirations take us—it's where we take our aspirations.

Turnarounds and transformations do not occur without culture change. Culture, in this context, means what the company or the team stands for and how its people operate among themselves and externally. Strong cultures are characterized by strong convergence and alignment around vision, mission, values and strategic direction. Changing culture starts by changing attitudes and behaviors. The linkage between attitude, behavior, culture and execution-driven performance has been validated in my own experience with not just one company but several. Therefore, in all chapters of this book, I will weave in background information and personal stories to accentuate the learnings of my Playbook. Throughout my career, I have repeatedly entered difficult situations—as a unit head, a division president, a group head of multiple divisions, a public-company CEO of three large global companies and, for almost the last three years, as chairman of a challenged global company. Again and again, my team and I applied the thoughts and practices from this Playbook to identify what was broken, to initiate turnarounds and to engineer transformations.

This Playbook applies the power of attitude, behavior and culture to three steps that lead to strategy excellence, executional excellence and enhanced productivity. Each step multiplies the benefits of the prior step, like compound interest. Start with *self-improvement*, then compound that by *improving people around you*, and then compound that by *improving the team*.

PRODUCTIVITY-ENHANCEMENT STEPS

Step 1: Make *yourself* stronger.
Step 2: Make *people around you* stronger.
Step 3: Make *the team* stronger.

As you will read in Chapter Six, these productivity-enhancement steps build on each other, resulting in a total productivity increase of up to twice that of the baseline.

This book is divided into two parts. The first part, Unleash the Power of *Me*, discusses how to make you and the people around you stronger. The second part, Unleash the Power of *We*, discusses how to improve the team as a whole. By design, there is overlap between the two parts because many of the elements of success that work on the individual also work on other people and the larger organization.

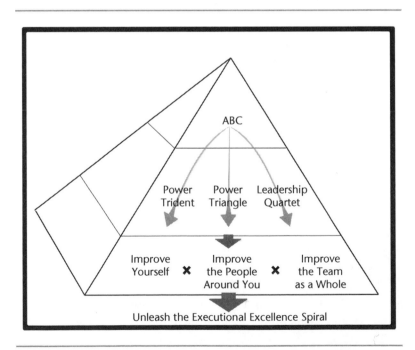

FIGURE I.2   The ABC Diffusion Pyramid of Serial Success

The ABC Diffusion Pyramid of Serial Success (Figure I.2) depicts the pathways that build a culture of enhanced productivity within an organization. At the top of the pyramid, ABC diffuses across the organization via three productivity-enhancing pathways: the Power Trident, the Power Triangle and the Leadership Quartet. (Each concept is more fully explained later in the book.) These pathways help unleash the Executional Excellence Spiral. (Also explained later in the book.)

As illustrated in Figure I.3, the Executional Excellence Spiral sustains and reinforces a company's transformation journey.

As productive cultures develop within an organization, they fuel better strategies and better executions, and they provide a competitive edge in innovation. This then leads to sustained performance which is significantly better than what might originally have been expected by those who followed the company. This kind of performance can change broken companies into long-lasting dynamic machines.

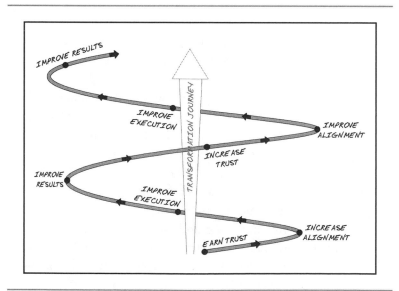

FIGURE I.3   The Executional Excellence Spiral

The ABC Advantage can be distilled into six change-leadership takeaways, each of which forms the basis for a chapter in this book.

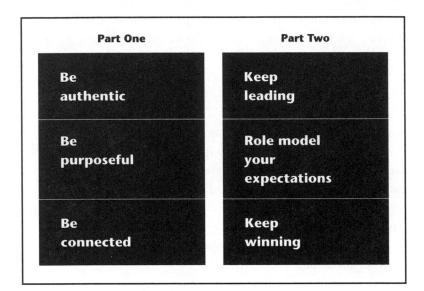

Part One	Part Two
Be authentic	**Keep leading**
Be purposeful	**Role model your expectations**
Be connected	**Keep winning**

In all my assignments, I worked hard at tapping the reservoir of human ability and attitude that exists in all of us. My team worked hard to get our people to adopt an attitude that would enable them to maximize their own potential and the potential of the people around them.

I learned early that reinvention and change leadership is a momentum game. In taking on tough situations, I made the case for change. I worked with teams simultaneously on multiple fronts. We focused on securing early wins, laying a foundation of positive attitudes and productive behaviors, articulating a journey, delineating the success markers, asking for sacrifices and aligning people on a common success path—then repeatedly reinforcing the execution via role modeling and messaging. Our activities on multiple fronts got change momentum to start building until it reached critical mass—then our sustained follow-through allowed the execution flywheel to be repeatedly reinforced. Had we not been hugely proactive at the front end, we would never have commanded the respect and the credibility that allowed people to unfreeze their attitudes and to buy into our change programs.

■ ■ ■

I often get asked, "What's the difference between this book and other books on change leadership?"

The biggest differentiator is that this Playbook places great importance on the CEO's personal role modeling with respect to being closely watched, judged and mirrored by the other members of the organization. Once members *personalize* with the CEO, and believe in him or her, they are ready to align, make sacrifices and provide extraordinary and sustained performance. Similarly, customers and partners are more energized by the CEO's authenticity and sense of urgency than by pronouncements of what he or she plans to do. This book is not as heavy on organizational strategy, mergers, acquisitions and restructurings as might be the case with many other titles on business or leadership.

The other big differentiator is that the strategies presented in this Playbook were proven via on-the-ground experiences on three continents and in six global companies. This broad base builds extra comfort into the ideas behind this book. Change leadership is more role modeling than business theory. It is more about venturing out, making sacrifices, taking risks, energizing teams around a common dream, coming back from adversity, relentlessly getting better, passionately executing and having fun as a winning team.

If done right, the rewards that this proven approach to change leadership can bring about are enormous—not just operationally and financially, but personally and professionally.

One

UNLEASHING THE POWER OF *ME*

How to Make Yourself and the People Around You Stronger

Part One of this book discusses how to make yourself and the people around you stronger. Its three major change-leadership takeaways are: *be authentic, be purposeful* and *be connected.*

The first change-leadership takeaway is to *be authentic.* Chapter One focuses on valuing integrity, knowing who you are and knowing what you want to do with your life.

The second change-leadership takeaway is to *be purposeful*. This is the subject of Chapter Two. Once you know what you want, develop clear goals, venture out, build energy and renew yourself periodically.

The third change-leadership takeaway, as discussed in Chapter Three, is to *be connected*, which moves beyond being connected with yourself to being connected with people around you and with your environment.

Chapter 1   Be Authentic

The first change-leadership takeaway is to *be authentic*. It begins with valuing integrity, knowing who you are and knowing what to do with your life.

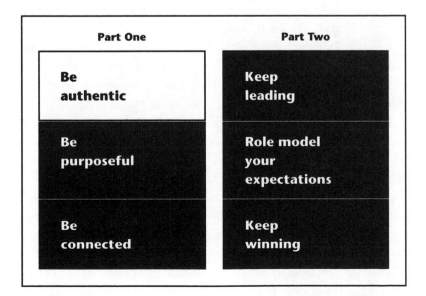

Part One	Part Two
Be authentic	Keep leading
Be purposeful	Role model your expectations
Be connected	Keep winning

LOOK IN THE MIRROR

When, in 1974, I moved from northern New Jersey to work at the Dorsey Laboratories Company in Lincoln, Nebraska (about as far from where I grew up as anywhere in the world), I understood how I might be perceived—as a foreigner with an accent in a suit sent from corporate. I was also only the second senior Sandoz executive to show up at this fiercely independent company, which had been taken over by Sandoz seven years earlier. Acknowledging that there would be all sorts of reasons for people to resent or be suspicious of me, I resolved to show them what I believed to be the real me—a down-to-earth person who wanted to make a difference.

Noreen and I acculturated with ease. Our positive attitudes made living in Nebraska enjoyable. We appreciated the warmth and hospitality of the new friends we made. We even became Cornhuskers fans and took in several home games, which were always amid a sea of red from the clothing of the enthusiastic fans chanting, "Go Big Red!"

At the office, I focused on listening, learning and making a difference. Within weeks, I knew I was gaining traction. I was getting invited in on important projects, such as the company's first five-year plan, and was soon promoted to the Operations Committee, Dorsey's *Team at the Top* that ran the company.

It was at Dorsey that I realized the collective teamwork and role modeling by the Team at the Top is critical as part of shaping a culture. That is why my Playbook uses this term repeatedly rather than conventional terms such as "Corporate Management."

I kept getting promoted every year or two until I became the top commercial person at Dorsey. Then, while in my mid-30s, I accepted the opportunity to run a country operation for Sandoz as the local CEO. At my farewell dinner in June 1980, I received a plaque from the Operations Committee that described the philosophy I follow and carry with me to this day: "Success begins by reinventing oneself—via self-awareness, self-knowledge, and self-development."

I had started developing my Playbook even before I went to business school, and now I was using and refining it—always starting with having a positive attitude (described in more detail later in the book). Building strength begins with having the courage to look into the mirror and to be brutally honest about what you see. You need to look in the mirror in order to recognize how people perceive you, so that you can then decide how to present yourself as you truly are. Positive transformation requires you to ask yourself the following questions: Who am I? What do I want? How am I doing? How am I *really* doing? How can I improve?

Learning self-truths via self-interrogation builds personal strength, which is necessary for building strength in others and for building team strength.

USE MIRRORS TO TELL THE TRUTH

In a crisis, getting people to honestly see themselves can help turn around a game that is going badly for the home team. Going into the crisis at Schering-Plough (SGP) in 2003, I wanted to do something to show our people that we were all in this together—that only through *their* efforts could Schering-Plough be saved.

Brent Saunders, whom I brought in as head of compliance, had mirrors mounted at principal sites around the company. (Brent later became CEO of Bausch + Lomb). The idea was to start changing the mindset of our people. Since the company was in serious hot water with federal investigators for a variety of compliance issues, one goal of the mirrors was a practical one: to convince people to alert us to issues we should know about. There was a telephone number posted just under the mirror so that people knew whom to call if they had a question on compliance, suspected wrongdoing or knew of even unintentional violations.

We were encouraging people to do the right thing, but the purpose of the mirrors was much more. At companies in crisis, people tend to feel victimized and send negative energy to the people around them. We wanted our people, especially our frontline people, to take ownership of both the problems *and* the solutions. We wanted people to see *themselves* as part of the answer, as opposed to looking at *others*. We wanted them to develop productive attitudes.

We hoped the person in the mirror staring back would say, "If you see bad things happening, *you* are responsible for doing something about them. If you see good things happening, recognize them too."

Self-honesty is an essential authenticity strength.

KNOW WHO YOU ARE NOT

Sometimes looking in the mirror can help you recognize your limitations. In 1991 I was heading up Wyeth Domestic and Wyeth R&D (research and development), and one of the tough calls I made was in the leadership of the R&D division. Productivity, especially in the *D* (development) area, had not kept up with the best-performing companies. We had a big hole in our late-stage new-product pipeline. In trying to replace the exited R&D chief, I flirted with some radical thoughts. I was considering breaking up Wyeth's R&D and having both research *and* development report to me directly. This way, I could focus on the development operations directly.

Bob Essner worked for me as head of commercial. (Bob later became chairman and CEO of Wyeth.) He had taken a chance on me by being the first to join me in 1989 at Wyeth from Sandoz U.S. I asked Bob for his opinion about my idea of taking direct control of both research and development. He responded with a question: "Are you comfortable being head of R&D?" This subtle question made me realize what Bob already knew—I was not an "R&D guy." Instead, I hired Bob Levy, MD, a world-renowned medical research leader, to head both *R* and *D*. He thrived in that position, and helped us build the strongest pipeline in Wyeth's history.

Another "know who you are not" leadership style I learned was to rely on the functional and technical experts to do their jobs. I didn't hesitate to pressure-test where I felt the need—but in the end, I wanted them to own their decisions.

Strong executives at every level of a company have mature and attuned attitudes that enable them to ask those they trust the tough questions about their abilities and their ideas—and to listen even if it isn't what they want to hear.

External feedback is important. Strong leaders must build a safe environment in which they can receive honest feedback from those around them. Besides recognizing your strengths, it is important to know when you need help from smart people. I know iconic CEOs who got derailed because they did not mitigate their own weaknesses with "A-players." I have always tried to have strong players on my team, whose strengths obviated weaknesses and whose skills were complementary to mine and the other players'. I have also tried to have sounding boards and advisers on various subjects both within and outside the companies where I work, and outside people who could be even more objective. Having people around you who become the yangs to your yin, who help you keep your feet on the ground, becomes even more important the higher up you go in an organization.

The higher up we go in the organization, the more we get work done through other people. This means not only building trust with the people who will execute our decisions, but also a willingness to let go of the control that we may have had as successful individual contributors.

We may be fiercely proud of our own accomplishments, but, as leaders, we take pride in the accomplishments of others.

By knowing who you are not, you can offset your weaknesses.

KNOW WHO YOU ARE

In addition to knowing who you are not, it is important to *know who you are*. I learned early in my career that I had a passion for and an ability to drive product innovation and global product launches. At Dorsey in the 1970s, I volunteered with corporate to launch a new antihistamine allergy medicine, Tavist. This medicine had already been launched in Europe. Even though the FDA had approved the product, Tavist had sat on the shelf for more than a year at Dorsey's then-larger sister division, Sandoz, because the Sandoz product-management group felt it was too difficult to launch. I got Dorsey Product Management busy with Tavist—but I also dug in as a "product driver." The creative sessions built energy and growing conviction. We launched Tavist within six months of it being assigned to us. Tavist sales and profits in the United States soon surpassed those in other territories. Corporate headquarters in Basel, Switzerland, was so surprised with our success that the CEO, Dr. Marc Moret, asked me to be a special speaker on the Tavist story at the company's centennial celebration in Basel in the fall of 1986.

Some important questions to ask yourself are: Do I have the natural talent to excel in the job to which I am aspiring? Am I willing to fail? Am I willing to be relentless in the face of disappointments? Where you are not sure about your abilities, my perspective has been that you should have a bias toward "I can do it." Believing in yourself makes you more likely to succeed.

You should try to find your hidden strengths, and then lead from them.

MAKE BUSINESS INTEGRITY A COMPETITIVE EDGE

Business integrity is a better working model than *ethics* or *morality.* The latter two are colored by the lens of the beholder, which sometimes reflects local religion or culture in a judgmental and divisive way. Business integrity is universal.

I learned from my parents that reputation and trust are critical. My dad retired in 1969. In 1976, the prime minister of Pakistan, Zulfikar Ali Bhutto, asked him to come out of retirement to be Pakistan's ambassador to India, and to reopen the embassy, which had closed after the 1971 war. Prime Minister Bhutto told my father that he was choosing him knowing that he did not belong to his political party, but knowing that my father's whistle-clean reputation would help him gain rapid acceptance by India's prime minister, Indira Gandhi. I saw my dad succeed as a leader in his field because he earned trust.

The Catholic schools I went to embedded in me the values of diversity of thought, self-learning and doing good to others. I remember two booklets that were a part of our curriculum, both of which made a lasting impression on me. One was called

Moral Science, and the other, *Hints on Politeness*. From them I learned that all human beings are special because they have intellect, memory, will and conscience. I learned that there were crosscutting basic values, such as the Golden Rule, that bring people together.

The fundamental premise is that we start life being morally equal—regardless of the family, the religion or the country we are born into. Through experience we refine our awareness of what is right or wrong until we become responsible for our own integrity. As CEO, I worked to develop a common language and understanding of business integrity that could span countries, cultures and religions. After my arrival at SGP, when the company was in serious hot water with the Department of Justice, one of my main messages at the first global town hall meeting in April 2003 was, "Let's look to business integrity as a way to *differentiate ourselves by earning trust.*"

Business integrity was commonly understood—whether we were in Kuala Lumpur, or Nanjing, or Prague, or Berlin, or New York, or São Paulo. The strong culture we developed made it possible to reenter into "compliance-challenged" countries like South Korea and Brazil, and to grow fast with our local operations there. SGP's Business Integrity Program became a learning center for other much larger companies.

Business integrity also means not playing favorites—even when we like someone more than others. Fairness builds trust. As CEO, I tried to be impartial not only on business matters, but also on social matters (such as not singling out any Level 2 colleagues for golf or card games or social trips).

All of us at one time or another, in both our careers and our private lives, will be confronted with decisions that will be guided by our own view of "doing the right thing." Business integrity will allow us to sleep well at night.

In the spring of 1997, I had already decided to leave Wyeth (WYE) to take the CEO job at Pharmacia & Upjohn (PNU) when Ulf Wiinberg, a global executive who we inherited as a result of the American Cyanamid acquisition in 1994, was offered a job by my *about-to-be* employer, PNU. PNU had a leadership hole to fill in Sweden, and Ulf, with his experience and Swedish background, would have been a perfect fit. But at Wyeth, I had him on our HTL (hate-to-lose) list, and I felt a responsibility to my *current* employer. We made a counteroffer to Ulf that kept him at Wyeth. Ulf, subsequently, did a great job running Wyeth's UK operation, Wyeth Consumer and Wyeth Europe, before taking a public-company CEO job in 2008. PNU never got Ulf, but I slept well at night.

Integrity is fundamental to serially successful leadership.

BE INSPIRED

I was the first person in my family to attempt an advanced science education. One day in 1960, I went to my physics teacher, Mr. Rogers (a British expatriate), and told him I wanted to drop his course. He said no. He told me I *had* ability and convinced me to keep trying. Seven years later, I majored in chemical engineering at the Imperial College of Science and Technology at the University of London.

When I look back on my high school years, I am grateful to Mr. Rogers. He wasn't a brilliant instructor or even a warm individual, but he told me that I had ability, that he believed in me and that he refused to accept my decision to drop his class. That inspired me.

By expecting and demanding a lot of ourselves, and by having clear goals, we inspire those around us.

Once you are inspired, think like a winner. Develop the mental muscle to build positivity. And if negativity arises, get rid of it—fast! Gain energy and strength by making a mental picture of what success will look like. Repeatedly visualize the destination with clarity, feeling and excitement.

Choose friends and companions who have positive attitudes, and who feed your aspirations, your commitment and your energy. Stay away from the "damp rags."

Be inspired, then inspire others.

BE HUMBLE

I learned early in my career about "the arrogance of success." After leading the dramatic turnaround of Dorsey Laboratories' Triaminic line of cough and cold products in 1976, my self-confidence soared. I went on to acquire a snazzy trade name, Sunbrella, and launched a new sunscreen product with that name. The product turned out to be a complete disaster! I had assumed that dermatologists would actively recommend the product to their patients to help them avoid skin cancer. What I didn't know was that the sunscreen category was largely a seasonal "push" business that required aggressive trade promotions primarily targeted to sun-soaked recreational areas. This was not Dorsey's business model! The inventory write-off was painful, but the failure taught me to look hard in the mirror and learn to temper self-confidence with humility.

Hubris is the number one reason that top leaders fail. Time and time again people lose perspective as they climb the corporate ladder.

When I, as a board member, see someone promoted to CEO, I look at how a former Level 2 person is now handling Level 1 power. Is she going out of her way to remain humble, or is she letting power dull her sense of who she really is? Is she still returning phone calls from those who contributed to her success?

It must be said that it is incumbent on a newly appointed CEO, especially one who has been promoted from within the company, to establish a certain *emotional distance* from former peers so that she can hold them accountable. She also needs to quickly earn the *legitimacy* that comes from attitude, behavior, raw competence and relentless energy. But it remains the case that executives need the attitude of humility to *actively* listen and *actively* learn, and to know that *what* is done and the *way* it is done can always be better.

I remember having a debate on ego and ambition in my early years at school. Channeled well, these can lead to tremendous advances for mankind (Thomas Edison is an example of an individual who channeled ego and ambition well). Channeled poorly, they can lead to horrific consequences for mankind (Adolf Hitler is an example of an individual who channeled ego and ambition poorly). Good leaders must have ego and ambition in order to have the drive and the commitment to stay the course. They also need to have humility, self-awareness and self-control so they can stay balanced and work well with people.

At Harvard Business School, I took a course that taught humility. We wrote WACs (written analyses of business cases) that were subsequently graded by liberal arts undergraduates at the neighboring all-women Wellesley College. They gave us in-person feedback on our analyses and written communications. The experience was often humbling. For the arrogant among us at Harvard (arrogance at Harvard, oh my!), there was the usual disdain: "What makes *them* qualified to be *our* graders?" But for most of us, who were learning about the importance of communicating complicated information simply and clearly, this was also a great exercise in humility.

I have tried to follow a questioning process of self-examination in order to prevent arrogance and maintain humility: Am I on the right path? Am I maintaining a sense of authentic humility? Am I acting with integrity? Am I owning my mistakes?

My parents modeled realistic behaviors like responsibility, modesty and frugality. "Keeping up with the Joneses" was an attitude that was pervasive when I was growing up during the 1950s. However, my family established its own comfort level. My parents sent my two siblings and me to Catholic schools where the fees were modest. Though the worn facilities reflected these modest fees, what mattered were the values and the discipline that the schools imparted, and the opportunity to work and play side by side with bright, hardworking kids from heavily subsidized households.

Building a frugal mindset early in life continued when my mother helped me open a savings account at the local post office and encouraged me to see the monthly accumulation in the account as a source of freedom and pride. I learned early that I can accomplish my goals with less. I also learned that people with simple needs are often happier than those who spend too much.

When I lived as a 19-year-old engineering student in London on $160 per month, and later, as an MBA student with Noreen in

Cambridge, Massachusetts, on $2,400 per year, I never felt disadvantaged, because there was always a way to live well and make the experience enjoyable.

Another important way to help you stay humble: keep your sense of humor. Connecting with oneself and with others is a human need, and, as leaders, we work hard at doing this well. A sense of humor always helps—it makes us more human. It provides a sense of perspective, and reminds us not to allow events to weigh us down. And it makes it easier to get in tune with colleagues and those we lead. It also helps create disarming moments during tough negotiation discussions. Even amid some failures, I tried to find humor as a way to motivate the team to learn and to move on.

Humility is a strength of serially successful leaders.

TAKE CHARGE, AND DON'T PLAY THE VICTIM

We must not become "victims," when, in fact, we can do a lot to take charge of our own destinies.

"My supervisor doesn't like me; he thinks I'm no good." This may or may not be true, but what are you going to do about it? Are you going to walk around saying "I've been pigeonholed" and wait for the ax to fall? I hope not. You control your psyche. You control your life. Don't play the victim. *Work to change the situation.* If you are passed over when you deserve the job, redouble your efforts. If the situation looks impossible, then for heaven's sake, leave as soon as practicable! If your environment is not favorable, then reinvent yourself and your environment.

I once worked in a company that had a famously autocratic culture. Some coworkers described it as almost intolerable. The finance department wielded excessive power. People were often verbally abused in an environment of bad language, excessive drinking and disrespect. I remember, for example, a written request—to spend $4,000 to send an A-player to a seminar—getting no reply. I later heard it went into the finance chief's wastebasket!

But I didn't let those things make me a victim. I opened up a comfort zone by not focusing on the negatives. I searched for good qualities and found the positives. The executives around me were financially driven and liked to do deals. I earned their trust by showing that I was good at not only making my operating numbers, but also at deal sourcing, deal negotiations and follow-through. I used my increasing credibility to empower those around me, making my environment more tolerable and productive. Not only was I able to help improve the environment, but I kept receiving extra responsibilities and promotions.

We must take ownership of what we do and the choices we make. We own our attitude. We own our happiness.

TAKE OWNERSHIP, SHUN THE BLAME GAME

Unfortunately, in business and politics, accountability often gets sidetracked by escapist behaviors like passing the blame, denial, justifying, passive-aggressiveness or outright giving up. Taking ownership of what I did was deeply embedded in me as an engineering student in my teens in London—a continent away from where I grew up—and as a newly married, recently arrived MBA student in Massachusetts. As CEO, I worked hard on setting a tone and relying on my Level 2s to also set the tone and to encourage the frontlines to do the right thing and to take ownership of what they did.

Just as one should never play the victim game, one should shun the blame game. It becomes counterproductive very fast. Take ownership of yourself and your actions. Taking ownership is all about accountability; it gives us the ability to be counted upon. Accountability includes positive behaviors like taking charge, being willing and embracing freedom. It means taking responsibility for change, both in your personal life and as a member of a team.

Accountability puts you in control, allowing you to take command of your attitude and behavior and to make things happen. It gives you that inner glow that comes from pride of ownership.

DEAL WITH WHAT STARES YOU IN THE FACE

When I became CEO of Pharmacia & Upjohn (PNU) in May 1997, job one was to untangle the mess created by the Swedish company Procordia AB's original acquisition of the Italian company Farmitalia Carlo Erba in November 1993, which resulted in the creation of Pharmacia, and its subsequent merger with Michigan's Upjohn in November 1995. Frustration and even despondency were setting in. Shortly after I arrived, Jack Lamberton, a well-known financial analyst, wrote, "Only a miracle can save this company."

As an outsider, I was able to identify the immediate problem soon after I took charge. The goal of the merger had been to create a unified global company with a powerful R&D and commercial engine. What had happened instead was that the merged company was structured to pacify the fiefdoms in Kalamazoo, Stockholm and Milan. Predictably, power struggles ensued and the new central "corporate" office in Windsor, UK, had neither the capability nor the will to step in and rectify the situation. A "decision by committee" with a "right to veto" environment was adding to the mess.

Why couldn't others see what was staring them in the face? There was too much wishful thinking that "things are going to be fine," too much complaining, commiserating, apathy or, in some cases, hopelessness and capitulation. But the primary culprit was defensiveness on the part of those who had put the merger together. The individuals who were protecting their turf dug in. The investors, too, were fearful of change, which could further harm the stock price in the short term.

We *saw* the problem and we were determined to *do* something about it. We moved with speed to break down the cultural divides that had fractured the company. We eliminated the three regional "business centers" in Kalamazoo, Stockholm and Milan, and created a single global organization with an operating headquarters that would have a stronger link to our 60 country operations. We reinvented the company's environment by moving the combined operations, including the U.S. commercial operations from Kalamazoo, to a new site in New Jersey. In the process, we

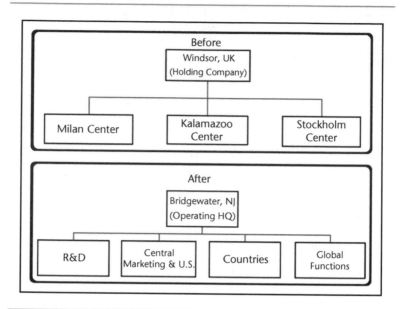

FIGURE 1.1 Pharmacia & Upjohn: Early Actions on Structure

eliminated management layers and encouraged sharing staff work between the U.S. operations and the global functions (such as having the product marketing function do both the global and the U.S. work). (See Figure 1.1 for the before and after constructs.)

The announcement was traumatic for many people who were faced with moving their families thousands of miles from home, or relocating for a second time within two years. But it was also greeted with relief by those who understood that only a radical fix could cure the dysfunction. Almost all of the executives who were invited to relocate from the "holding company" headquarters in Windsor to New Jersey did so. In their hearts, they knew it was the right decision.

After the reorganization, we made a conscious choice to go global with our commercial engine. We united behind five high-potential products for the newly globalized organization. We wanted these "product drivers" to be properly introduced and maximized in as many of our 60 country operations as possible. I sat in on many R&D presentations, where our newly globalized R&D team searched for the best new-product bets, and removed those that were less promising. We made the infighting and the paralysis irrelevant by completely changing the dynamic of our now reinvented company. We wrested control of our most important R&D projects and our globally promoted products from the regional fiefdoms, and put them into the hands of simplified global teams and our country managers. We also reduced the corporate management team from nineteen to seven, and, in the process, eliminated many senior leaders who were culture resistors. We had a "very low tolerance for the energy absorbers, the loners, the politicians, the silo operators, and the malcontents."[1]

By 1998, PNU had experienced a dramatic turnaround, making possible transformational actions such as the acquisition of the oncology company Sugen in 1999, and the Monsanto mega-merger in 2000. We morphed from a $15-billion market cap company in 1997 to a $52-billion market cap company three years later upon PNU's merger with Monsanto.

When I faced difficult starting points, my Playbook was almost always to make people confront the unwelcome truths of the situation we were facing at that time. Then it was to ask people to make a commitment to change and to making sacrifices; to identify what needed to change, communicate it to stakeholders and get buy-in; make the tough calls and then get the entire team to move forward in the same direction and with a sense of purpose.

Face reality and face it fast.

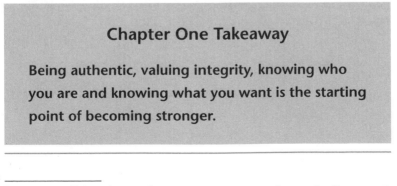

Chapter One Takeaway

Being authentic, valuing integrity, knowing who you are and knowing what you want is the starting point of becoming stronger.

[1]Victoria Griffith, "The People Factor in Post-Merger Integration," *strategy+business*, Third Quarter 2000/Issue 20.

Chapter 2 Be Purposeful

The second change-leadership takeaway is to *be purposeful*. Once you know what you want, develop clear goals, venture out, build energy and renew yourself periodically.

Part One	Part Two
Be authentic	**Keep leading**
Be purposeful	**Role model your expectations**
Be connected	**Keep winning**

USE THE RULE OF 3S

Priority setting and sequencing activities are crucial to a purpose-driven life. I learned early that when faced with a lot, I must always ask myself, "What are the three areas of focus that will get me the most yardage toward where I am going?" This is what I call the Rule of 3s.

Once the priorities are clear, follow up relentlessly as you move in the direction you want to go. Wherever possible, gain extra leverage by delegating to those you trust.

The Rule of 3s works well in many aspects of your life and your career—for example, in time management. Follow the Rule of 3s to prioritize your day. Daily prioritization is especially necessary when times become more turbulent. The "urgent" often gets mixed up with the "important." Both require careful allocation of time.

During the 1980s, we began our marketing planning process at Sandoz by first determining which of our products would gain the most traction for our promotional dollars (also known as promotional return on investment [ROI], or return on promotional investment). We selected three products for full funding. The managers of the products getting the full funding were expected to develop extensive plans so that they would be *winning* plans. The product managers receiving fewer resources would be saved from the "busywork" of developing programs that would not be getting the funding they would typically request. For those products receiving fewer resources, we had their product managers create marketing plans on a limited scale. Besides saving time, we were also able to save headcount, as we could limit the number of people dedicated to these less critical products. This focus on strategic thrusts allowed us to center our attention on areas where our company and our leaders could excel.

Fighting clutter, assigning priorities and focusing resources are important to building a sense of purpose.

USE THE POWER TRIDENT

The Power Trident has been my inner driver in building strength. The Power Trident comprises the three prongs of *Passion, Courage* and *Tenacity* (Figure 2.1).

Passion is an investment we make in what we do. It can be an exhilarating feeling when we put our heart, body and soul into something we believe in. Enjoy your work and have passion for it. Put passion into what you are trying to achieve. Life is *now*. Every day matters. Be in a high-energy learning mode and concentrate on relentless follow-through every day. Say it, then do it. Doing things with passion is fun.

In March 2007, SGP announced the acquisition of Organon BioSciences for €11 billion. Only four months earlier, this 64-year-old "crown jewel" of the Dutch pharmaceutical industry saw Pfizer walk away as its major funding partner for its main R&D product, Saphris (asenapine). This medication had shown promise for treating both bipolar disorder and schizophrenia. However, brain research is exceptionally difficult, and this research compound had been languishing

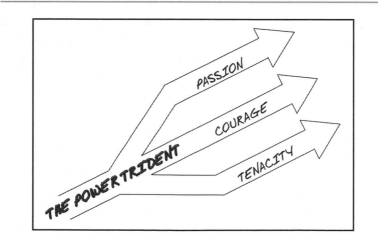

FIGURE 2.1 The Power Trident

in late-stage trials for years. In fact, during our acquisition conversations, our external advisers had placed little or no value on it. But after getting to know the researchers who had developed Saphris, we were impressed by their commitment to creating a drug to combat these serious and difficult-to-treat mental disorders. Their passion for Saphris made us think that this drug just might make it to the market. We, the senior leadership, tuned in to the researchers' commitment and lent our energy to their project. Surprisingly, our motivated team was soon able to resolve the obstacles and move the product through a "first cycle approval" at the FDA. Today it is one of the few, if not only, medications to have been introduced in the United States with *both* bipolar disorder and schizophrenia in the initial label. To a large degree, we succeeded because, by tuning in to the R&D team's sense of higher purpose, we unleashed the energy and motivation necessary to find a solution.[1]

Courage is the second attitudinal prong of the Power Trident. It allows us to leave our comfort zone and do what we believe is the right thing. We need courage in order to make the tough calls. *Few big changes can be accomplished without courage.*

One aspect of courage is to have candor, particularly in groups. I work hard at fighting "groupthink" when it comes to making judgments or developing strategies and action plans. In fact, I will often call on one member of the team to deliberately give another point of view so the entire team working on a project can hear another side before a decision is made. We want to know about the *consequences* and *risks* of what we are about to decide, *before* we decide it.

Sometimes courage requires us to be candid with ourselves about whether our attitude concerning the job at hand is aligned with the attitude that is required by the company. If these respective attitudes are out of alignment, changes have to be made. Neither obedience nor defiance is a good idea. A better idea is to undertake some soul-searching and, if necessary, careful conversations with

---

[1] The Saphris story originally appeared in "The Frontline Advantage" by Fred Hassan, published in *Harvard Business Review*, May 2011.

the right people. If you still don't feel aligned, then you should find another mission to get behind.

Tenacity, the third attitudinal prong of the Power Trident, requires the willpower to *stay the course* in the face of resistance and fatigue, and to persevere because you are *committed* to what you are doing.

We learn tenacity in different ways throughout our lives. For me, one early challenge was overcoming a serious stutter during my childhood. The fear of an oncoming stutter created a cycle of terror that worsened the stutter. I would practice and practice every day to build up my confidence so I could speak without pause. Sometimes you just have to keep trying until you get it right. Later, I realized that the same approach works when confronting tough situations in life or business:

- Put the problem into perspective.
- Don't panic; keep a cool head.
- Seek help and collaboration.
- Break up the challenge into bite-size pieces.
- Sustain your *winning attitude* as you go about solving each component of the problem.

Passion, courage and tenacity keep us going until we get there. We remain committed—with our heads and our hearts—to giving our best.

ENTER THE DISCOMFORT ZONE

I discovered early in my life that entering the *discomfort zone* can be not only exciting but also helpful in building self-confidence and vision. Entering this zone means to venture out, to face unknowns and to strive harder.

When I was growing up, I heard many stories of discomfort from my mother. She grew up in the desert, 300 miles from the large city of Lahore, her family's previous home. Her father—a pioneer with lots of courage but not much money—went into the desert and, once a canal was constructed for irrigation, built a thriving farm there. My mother, home tutored, obtained her "matriculation certificate," then headed north to Lahore where she attended Kinnaird College, run by Christian missionaries. She undertook a journey made by few women in the late 1920s. She proceeded to get her master's degree, ran successfully in the Pakistani elections of 1951 and became an advocate for and champion of women's causes. The most important lesson she passed on to me was that I should leave my comfort zone early in life. "If you live a life outside yourself," she told me, "you grow. If you live a self-absorbed life, you are limited in experience, vision and expertise."

In 1964 I set out in London to expand my expertise. The news that I was going to the UK and attending the Imperial College of Science and Technology was not as surprising to my family as the fact that I was confronting the "dreaded" sciences, a field no family member had studied before. I picked Imperial College because its fees were heavily subsidized in those days (i.e., they were very low cost compared to U.S. science schools), and because it was a tough school. Imperial College had a "meat-grinder school" reputation as evidenced by a high first-year failure rate. Although it was hard, uncomfortable work, by the time I graduated in 1967, the "science is not in our family" attitude was gone.

Engineering had given me an understanding of how to get things done, and a mental discipline to help me analyze, organize and execute. Additionally, I knew that an understanding of chemistry, physics and math would later give me the ability to trust my gut on decisions that would come my way in the later career I was planning—pharmaceuticals.

In the UK, exotic summer jobs helped me to accelerate my acculturation to a different land. At a chemical engineering facility in Kent in 1965, my job was to hose off the spray-dried egg from the vessel walls, which smelled like, well, rotten egg. Every day on the train ride back to my apartment from work, I stayed as far away as possible from the other passengers. Another summer, before I was promoted to chef, I picked gooseberries in Cambridgeshire with students from many European countries. In Cheshire, I worked in Shell's oil refinery, where I first saw that the frontline supervisor is the key to workers' motivation and morale.

The next discomfort I pursued was to be the first member of my family to go into "the business world." Business excited me because there were fewer constraints compared to my family's home base in civil service, and I felt I could find my own way there.

My first job out of college in 1967 was as a sales manager at the Lahore headquarters of a fertilizer company based out of Delaware that was affiliated with Hercules. Hercules, along with a Pakistani firm, Dawood, was building a huge fertilizer plant near Lahore. My sense of purpose came from being part of the Green Revolution, which included new seed varieties that were dramatically increasing yields in wheat, rice and cotton, which in turn needed the product I was selling—fertilizer. I was doing well there, and Pakistan was much calmer and more focused on economic development than what one reads now in the popular press. But Noreen and I both looked in the mirror and decided that adventure was more important than comfort. So, in September 1970, 18 months after we were married, we were on a Pan Am flight into Boston's Logan Airport.

Noreen and I had decided that business education would create bigger horizons, so I had enrolled in Harvard Business School. We took two suitcases—half of one filled with books that I thought might be useful. We arrived in Cambridge, Massachusetts, in a daze—but thankful—as three plane hijackings had just occurred in the Middle East and Europe. Airports at that time were still asleep regarding passenger security checks, and people were understandably nervous.

Everything was new to us. We had never seen a plastic shield protecting a cab driver before. The cab driver said to me, "You look fine, you can ride in the front." This welcome to the United States was reassuring, and my excitement about attending business school in this country was high. That first night we slept on the curtains, and we resolved to buy some used furniture the next day.

A few months later, the snow was deep and still falling as I walked among the sprawling Harvard University buildings dropping off advertising posters as my part-time job. Noreen, too, was busy, spending the long, dark evenings attending classes for her master's degree in early childhood education at Wheelock College. Neither the weather nor the austerity bothered us. We were enjoying living out of our comfort zone and knowing that, together, we were shaping our future.

The following summer of 1971, rather than looking for the usual staff job for MBA students, I chose a "shoe leather" sales job that was customer focused and quota driven. I sold consumer pharmaceuticals for Vicks (now part of Procter & Gamble), calling on pharmacies in an area just north of Manhattan, including tough areas in the Bronx, as well as some of the leafy suburbs of New York City. For me, entering a new culture, I couldn't think of a faster way to learn how to assimilate. I had to get people I had never met to trust me enough to buy what I was selling, or, at the very least, open the door, accept my outstretched hand and talk to me. At one South Bronx pharmacy, I was greeted by a leaping German shepherd whose chain stopped the animal inches from my nose. At a pharmacy in Yonkers, the pharmacist kept the doors locked and buzzed me in only after checking who I was. Every day was a new learning experience. It was exciting to be in the United States feeling free, dynamic, competitive and wonderful!

I would not have been able to bring the kind of change to the companies I led had I remained only in chemical engineering or in a single country.

Seeking out the discomfort zone forces learning and experience that can be put to good use in future challenges.

PRACTICE ACTIVE LEARNING

Successful executives are aggressive lifelong learners. They take joy in learning. One active-learning tool I began to practice at an early age was to test myself after reading an interesting report by asking myself a few pertinent questions and writing down the answers, sometimes on the back of an envelope. Then, I would go back to the original text and determine my hits and misses. And where I *missed*, I'd be sure to learn the answer. It takes extra time, but the lessons become etched more powerfully in your mind.

Another behavior-modeling practice I have followed for many years has been to write up a brief trip report on observations, learnings and suggested next steps after every significant visit to a country operation, site or professional conference. These reports helped me build a useful knowledge base, which I was able to refer to when visiting the same place or event the next time. I also readily shared this information. Putting my senior colleagues on a confidential mailing list not only improved information fluidity, but it also encouraged those colleagues to write and share their own trip reports. As a team at the top, we were extraordinarily well plugged into the operations.

Sometimes by doing my fast reads through volumes of paper—especially over weekends—I was able to see certain changes that may not have been widely seen at that time. Before doing the Monsanto deal in late 1999, for example, I did a fast read of the proceedings of the extensive Advisory Committee meetings organized by the FDA commissioner, Dr. Jane Henney, on foods based on genetically modified organisms (GMOs). These proceedings reinforced my conviction that the media frenzy surrounding this subject should not deter us from moving forward. We became the only Big Pharma to touch the GMO hot potato that was Monsanto. The resulting low premium made it a good deal.

Another macro trend I was able to identify by actively listening and learning was the hollowness of the dot-com boom, which was at its height in early 2000—the very time we were trying to sell the Monsanto investors on our Monsanto deal. Many Monsanto investors were angry at the low-premium offer from PNU, and there was speculation that the merger might fall apart—just as had happened with Monsanto's previously announced merger with Wyeth. We continued to communicate the positive business fundamentals of the deal—good strategic fit, good scientific fit and good revenue and cost-avoidance synergies. I went out of my way to compare this cash-flow-intensive deal favorably to the then "in favor" high-flying Internet stocks whose valuations could not be justified based on their cash flows. The sharp market correction for these Internet stocks began one month after *In Vivo* magazine published my observations in its February 2000 edition. In fact, between March 2000 and October 2002, $5 trillion of market value evaporated. Meanwhile, the PNU and Monsanto deal was closed on March 31, 2000. I attended the New York Stock Exchange ceremony celebrating the start of this new Big Pharma company. The newly formed PHA stock was born in strength.

Having supervised tens of thousands of talented employees (including hundreds of PhDs and MDs), the one correlation that became clear to me was that those who had the passion and the curiosity to learn had a huge advantage. Those who committed to becoming experts in their own areas and also to learning about the big picture—including the historical aspects of the country, the company or the technology they were working on—were able to develop the critical thinking and the judgment to do superior work.

Be curious and enjoy active learning.

GO GLOBAL

In the coming decades, the biggest growth in the world economy will continue to come from *outside* the United States. Many large, domestic-centric U.S. corporations would be wise to benefit from taking a global attitude.

A global attitude and mindset will enhance and build personal ability. Ask for assignments overseas early in your career. Ask for them not in terms of "check the box" foreign rotations, but in terms of real challenges and real risks if you don't perform. In my case, becoming a mini-CEO in an outlying country like Pakistan meant more management responsibility than in most countries. I think an early career rotation to the Philippines or Ukraine or Venezuela or Pakistan or Indonesia is more meaningful than being rotated as head of a large "less foreign" country like England, Canada or Australia. The lack of support systems from the center forces accelerated hands-on learning. As head of Sandoz Pakistan, I got to *do* more and *learn* more from the ground up.

Once overseas, try to get out of the comfort zone of the expat ghetto. Learn about the local history and the traditions of the place in which you're living. Engage with the locals. Connect with the local frontline managers and motivate people toward high performance.

Attitude, more than experience, makes a culture global. Putting people in foreign settings doesn't automatically imbue new attitudes. Recruiting people with the "right" education doesn't guarantee that people have the "right" attitude. I've met many people who speak three or four languages, yet still have a narrow view of the world. At the same time, I've come across people who speak only English, but who have a real passion and curiosity about the world and are effective in different cultures.

Having a global attitude means being sensitive to local customs— and being yourself wherever possible. I spent 17 years working for a Swiss company, but living primarily in the United States. In the 1970s, it was usually considered forward in Switzerland to address people by their first names. While I would address my senior Swiss executives using their last names, with my peers and subordinates I followed the more familiar U.S. standard. People were okay with this because they knew I was not being false. Being yourself, while also showing interest and openness, is at the heart of a global attitude.

By reinventing themselves as *authentic* global players, U.S. companies can capture their share of the profit migration to the newer geographies. At SGP, our "one company, one culture, one team" motto made us a high-performance global business. More than half of our growth from $9 billion to $21 billion in sales during my six-and-a-half years at SGP came from foreign markets, and much of that from emerging markets.[2] We defined "global" not as force-fitting an American culture onto another country's operations. Instead, we *over*-defined global as being strong locally, yet tightly networked as one global team. By "localizing the global" in each country, we showed our respect for individual countries and gained "insider status" as a trusted *local* corporate citizen. We built a surprisingly powerful global culture for a historically U.S.-centric corporation.

---

[2] Operational (i.e., non-GAAP) numbers.

One place, for example, where we put this Playbook to work was in Turkey, which at the time was stereotyped as a mysterious and difficult country. We stopped sending expats there. Instead, we appointed Muti Bilgutay, an A-player, as country manager in 2003. He assembled a great team on the ground. He built trust in the city of Ankara. People were startled when the country's operation zoomed past $100 million annual sales in a very short period of time.

One important difference that helped strengthen SGP's global culture was the implementation of a "strong global, strong local, strong matrix" model, as opposed to the conventional U.S. company model of regional silos that run the countries, and a "domestic" silo in the U.S. Conventional companies work with three heavily staffed layers—corporate, regional and country headquarters. Not only is this costly, but country managers feel disempowered and bogged down with the slow movement of information and decisions. Our new model eradicated the layers of regional staff, separating country operations from their global-headquarter colleagues.

SGP's model, while more difficult to work initially, greatly improved the company's traction *inside* where the money was made—*in the individual countries*. Don't get me wrong: SGP had excellent regional managers.[3] They, however, saw their main job as attracting, retaining, coaching and supporting a cadre of A-players to run their assigned countries. Building overhead and staff at the regional headquarters was *not* their priority. Producing *business results inside their assigned countries* was what mattered.

That's the essence of an effective global company. The territory is the important building block, and the respective manager is in charge and accountable. But the manager must also contribute as part of a global network and must feel a strong sense of belonging to that network.

---

[3] Many of SGP's regional managers later moved on to much higher levels in other companies. For example, Francesco Granata, head of Western Europe/Canada, went on to become chief commercial officer at Biogen after SGP's merger with Merck in 2009.

A strong global culture goes beyond country managers. In September of 1999, I had my customary CEO dialogue with some of PNU's local sales reps in Jinan, a provincial town in China. I mentioned that we were rolling out a new stock option program to our sales representatives around the world, and I saw their eyes immediately light up.

The money or the stock didn't matter to them as much as the knowledge that they were receiving some of the same incentives as our U.S. reps, and therefore that they were being seen as valued colleagues.[4] We were one of the very early U.S. companies to give stock options to sales reps in emerging markets. At all the global companies I ran, we emphasized having locals run the countries wherever possible. Still, we did have a global community of expatriates to allow us flexibility in some countries. For this expat group, we guided them to certain attitudes and behaviors that would enable them to be more effective. (These are listed in Appendix E.)

Good ideas can come from anywhere. The more places with which you are familiar, the more ideas you will get and the more ideas you will benefit from.

Developing a global attitude is a distinctive strength in the twenty-first century.

BUILD COMPETENCE IN EMERGING MARKETS

In most industries over the coming decade, the overall growth rate in emerging markets will be more than three times faster than the overall growth of North America, Western Europe and Japan. However, the large domestic market makes it a challenge for many of my U.S. executive colleagues to reinvent their attitude toward the lesser markets. For example, a $30-million annual business in Colombia is not very exciting if the U.S. is $1 billion. Yet there are many "Colombias" out there and, over the long term, they are likely

---

[4] Part of this global discussion was originally published as an interview in "In Search of Global Leaders," *Harvard Business Review*, August 2003.

to grow faster than the United States. Also, the broader the country portfolio, the less the single-country risk.

Wintry weather had already arrived when I showed up at the Buenos Aires offices of Wyeth Argentina in 1993. The office had a slimmed-down look and employees were wearing heavy sweaters to fight off the chill. More importantly, the local company was fighting to survive; it had taken costs out, including lowering the thermostat, to fight the vicious economic downturn. Many other U.S. companies had fled Argentina altogether. Wyeth held firm. I saw passion, courage and tenacity among the employees of Wyeth Argentina. I knew we were going to make it—and we did.

Early in this century, I got to see another downturn in Argentina. In mid-December 2001, a million people took to the streets to protest economic conditions. Presidents came and went after very short tenures. Now it was Monsanto Argentina's turn to face the tough times. Monsanto remained loyal to a country that had been an early adopter of its agricultural biotech-based soybean seeds. Costs were cut and credit to customers was tightened. Monsanto Argentina stayed and made it through.

Many American companies tend to enter emerging markets late and move out early when times get tough. The more globalized European competitors tend to be better at seeing "beyond the valleys." It costs a lot more to reestablish when normality returns, so those companies that stay the course during difficult times will come out ahead. The difference in market shares and the long-term local profits becomes the scorecard for those who have a global mindset versus a conventional operating model.

My attitude toward emerging markets remained strong at all the companies I went to. Through returning to countries like Brazil and South Korea—more than a dozen new emerging countries in total—SGP, by 2009, had 12 percent of sales coming from the newly entered emerging markets, up from almost nothing just a few years earlier!

Global companies are good at differentiating *between* the emerging markets. South Korea is not the same as Indonesia; Argentina is very different from Vietnam. Individual emerging markets can look like a cup half full or half empty. Leaders with a global attitude generally look at the cup as half full, but also know how to act in each specific country.

Differentiate yourself from your competition by building a special competence in emerging markets.

MAKE DECISIONS WITH LESS-THAN-PERFECT INFORMATION

Becoming stronger as a leader means knowing when to stop analyzing and start doing. Going repeatedly into broken and complex situations, I had to hone this skill in order to get change momentum to become visible well before my "grace period" had expired. I have seen many managers who did not live up to their potential because they struggled with making decisions. They kept looking for more and more information and analyzing the data they received. Analysis paralysis can become a cultural affliction in big companies unless the CEO and his or her team at the top actively work to build this decision-making courage into their managers. Good leaders know when to stop the information churn and either say "no" or say "yes" and mobilize the team to move forward with purpose. They know that in most cases "perfect inaction" is not as good as "less-than-perfect action."

The leader's team must collect information, analyze the information, look at the quality of the information, develop options, recommend, decide—and then *execute*. At SGP, we tried to build into the business culture a practice of doing *homework* and *offline discussions* so that most meetings could either end with a decision, or information could be requested so that the next meeting would be decisive.

Cultural contrasts about decision-making processes among large companies can be huge. I know of companies where people feel so constrained by their own cultures that I keep hearing them say, for example, "The second meeting feels like the *beginning* of a decision-making process with no clear end in sight." Companies should avoid the tendency to process decisions without adequately separating out the ones that need a more deliberate approach from the ones that middle managers or front-line managers should be able to appropriately anchor, then decide on and move forward.

Especially in a crisis situation, the team must be good at managing ambiguity and moving with speed. Sometimes one has to make a choice between two unknowns, and sometimes between two "not very nice" alternatives. When time is limited, I try to get going by developing a hypothesis about what needs to be done. I then follow the loop of testing that hypothesis by piloting it, then observing, then iterating, then doing more, then scaling up the success formula that may have been uncovered. Leaders should have a bias for solving problems and seizing opportunities—even if they have to proceed empirically.

Making timely decisions makes you a better leader.

EMBRACE CHALLENGES

Challenges create excitement and energy. After arriving in Lincoln, Nebraska, in June of 1974, I surprised people by making a point of learning everything I could about Dorsey Laboratories' products, customers and competitors, and its R&D, manufacturing and commercial operations. I enrolled in a weeklong sales training class! I was a senior executive reporting to the head of the company, yet I wanted to learn the business from the ground up and as fast as possible.

I learned a lot at Dorsey about turnaround and transformation. In 1979 I was in the middle of venturing out of a comfort zone. My team was expanding our marketing for the Triaminic cough and cold products from a target market of about 100,000 doctors to 90 million TV households, and also expanding distribution from 50,000 pharmacies to food stores, mass merchandisers and other outlets that numbered in the hundreds of thousands.

In the middle of all this, Sandoz CEO Marc Moret, intrigued by my unusual degree of progress and wanting to test me again, asked me to take charge of the company's most challenged country operation, Sandoz Pakistan. It was tempting, since being asked to join the vaunted corps of Sandoz country managers represented an important promotion, but I declined, mainly because I was on a fast learning curve of understanding consumer behavior and consumer marketing. I also didn't want to miss the payoff. However, the situation with Sandoz's investment in its operating company in Pakistan was getting more desperate, and the following year (1980) Mr. Moret asked me again to take charge of Sandoz Pakistan and solve its problems, again expecting a turndown.

This time I felt differently, despite the fact that my friends and colleagues thought I was crazy for even contemplating the move. Dorsey's chief was particularly emphatic. "The Soviets have invaded Afghanistan and are looking to establish a warm-water port, and our president has bungled the helicopter mission to free the hostages in Iran," he argued. "Why would you want to go to that part of the world?" But I was up for the challenge. I knew that being given total accountability for a country operation *anywhere* in the world would give me invaluable experience. But I had another reason, which I kept mostly to myself. After I accompanied my mother to two major surgeries at Memorial Sloan-Kettering Cancer Center in New York, her esophageal cancer had returned, and she was now living alone in Pakistan. My father had passed away three years earlier.

Taking the Sandoz Pakistan assignment turned out to be one of my best decisions. I did get to see my mother for a few weeks. She held Noreen's hand as she passed away—with my siblings and me nearby. I was a mini-CEO at the age of 35, in charge of sales, marketing, manufacturing, quality, new-product development, government relations, finance, legal and human resources. I was able to learn and do practically all the aspects of a general management role. Also, being a country manager allowed me to become a global-organization insider, and allowed me to broaden my worldview.[5]

After making the case for change, building trust and change momentum were the key as I set about the task of saving the Sandoz Pakistan operation. I again used my Playbook formula to energize the frontline managers. I moved many senior people out and made sure the new ones I brought in were A-players with the right attitude and with a track record of excellence in their assigned functions. The role modeling by this new team at the top assisted me in getting the needed traction. My best hire, Dr. Farid Khan, was for the "hardest to fill" job—to take charge of the sophisticated manufacturing complex we had in a remote desert location. I managed to hire him away from the manufacturing operation he successfully ran in Karachi, a much more desirable location. Although the German pharmaceutical company he was working for, Hoechst AG (now part of Sanofi), tried hard to keep him, I convinced him he could make a bigger difference at Sandoz. He joined me in embracing challenges!

At Sandoz Pakistan, I got to work with groups that corporate executives in more developed markets tend to stay away from. The unions had been staging slowdowns at the manufacturing plant, and I spent a lot of time with them listening to their grievances and to their ideas. We had fun together and that made a difference—I ran a three-legged race in one of their social events to show that I was a person they could relate to. More importantly, I shared with them my strategy for the company, and showed them that their jobs could thrive only if we all worked together to make the company strong.

When, several months later, my CFO colleague, Otto Schurmann, gave me the good news that our country operation's profits had finally moved into strong and safe territory, I startled the union membership by showing up at the plant and announcing their first-ever annual bonus to celebrate the new era of profitability. They had never had a chance to negotiate for a bonus due to the poor profitability—so this unexpected gesture accelerated trust building.

I also made sure that we were viewed as a trusted member of the community. One of my most fulfilling moments in that job was the construction of a water pipe from the manufacturing plant to an adjacent village. For the first time in this unforgiving and brutally hot desert area, villagers had access to clean, filtered water—from a pharmaceutical plant's water system, of all places! At the inauguration ceremony, they offered to name the village after me, but that was obviously not appropriate. It still felt good.

Sandoz Pakistan's culture changed dramatically. Quality, productivity and margins all began to rise. Sales climbed fast. Our early turnaround results started a cascade of trust building that resulted in even more positive results. The virtuous spiral, which I call the Executional Excellence Spiral, kicked in beautifully. The culture there became so strongly transformed that the country operation became a "learning center" within the Asia-Pacific region, with people as far away as New Zealand coming to observe and learn. We developed a set of slides so that we could share our global Playbook with others.

The turnaround results at Sandoz Pakistan were stunning to corporate headquarters in Basel, Switzerland. In three years we jumped five places in rankings in the Pakistan market, and earnings went from losses to matching earnings from some of Sandoz's mid-tier European country operations. So stunning were the results that I was given the opportunity to run Sandoz U.S. well before my planned tenure at Sandoz Pakistan was completed. Sandoz U.S. was the *largest* operation of the company.

Embracing challenges greatly helped me build and reinforce my leadership Playbook.

REINVENT YOURSELF AND YOUR ENVIRONMENT

I repeatedly sought to reinvent myself by taking on assignments, not just to advance my career, but also for the intrinsic rewards of experiencing new functions (sales, marketing, R&D, manufacturing, planning), new businesses (agriculture, chemicals, veterinary, devices, consumer) and, of course, new locations (on-the-ground jobs on three continents).

Wading into the discomfort zone only once is usually not enough. Many of us reinvent ourselves every five or so years. If, at the same time, we get to reinvent our environment, that can be even more fulfilling. I often elected to reinvent myself even when I was happy in my current environment.

"This must be what divorce feels like," I said to Noreen in January 1989. Word had gotten out to the Sandoz CEO, Marc Moret, that I was "destabilized" (accepting outside approaches to talk about my next career move), so he sent an invitation for me to come see him in Lausanne, Switzerland. Yes, I *had* been destabilized—I had already given my word to Jack Stafford, CEO of Wyeth, to take over its domestic pharmaceuticals division, and I didn't think it would be right to invite a counteroffer once I had given my word.

Why leave Sandoz after 17 years when things were going so well for me, where I had so many boosters and friends, and where I had earned the trust and respect of the corporate leadership? In the first place, it was a conscious decision to reinvent myself again after five fulfilling years of transforming the company's largest operation, its U.S. subsidiary. And secondly, Sandoz was now sounding me out about yet another promotion that would now move me to corporate headquarters in Switzerland. I could not ask Noreen to move overseas at that time.

Arriving at Wyeth's sprawling Pennsylvania facilities in February 1989, I saw the huge—and exciting—challenge. This New York–headquartered company, which had been number one in global Big Pharma only a few years earlier, was suffering from the patent expiry of two important drugs. The first was Ativan, prescribed for anxiety; and the second, Inderal, prescribed for high blood pressure. On top of that, its most successful product, the mare-urine-derived estrogen drug Premarin (for menopause-related conditions), was about to be challenged by the arrival of a synthetic generic mixture. The generic competitor was so confident in the success of its drug that it had stocked introductory supplies in warehouses—ready to go.

Another difficult issue was the usual personnel challenges that accompany an internal merger—this one between Wyeth and Ayerst, which had occurred in 1987. Two of the senior commercial people, one from legacy Wyeth and the other from Ayerst, had just been terminated. Former Ayerst people confided in me about being "taken over" by Wyeth, while legacy Wyeth people had their own concerns. Tribalism was rife, and there were even allegations of dirty tricks.

Coming in to this tough environment, I used my Playbook formula. Convince people of the need for change. Build trust and change momentum. Listen and learn. Reach out to the frontline managers. Pick a good Team at the Top. Expect each member of this team to be very good at what they do, *and*, at the same time, expect them to be good team players and role models. Expect passion, courage and tenacity from each member of the team, and expect members to *collectively* model innovation, speed and flexibility. Then get them to set winning strategies and relentlessly lead the follow-through.

At Wyeth, assembling a good Team at the Top was a crucial ingredient in tackling the company's problems head-on. One of the team's earliest tasks, for example, was to reach out to women's patient groups, key medical leaders and the FDA and to present our argument that a synthetic copy of Premarin should not be considered identical to Premarin. We believed the facts were on our side, since Premarin's mix of ingredients uniquely came from the urine of pregnant mares. It is rare for the FDA to backtrack, especially if there is political pressure, which there was a lot of in this case. Good science won on this occasion, and, to this day, Premarin remains uncopied.

Over the next eight years, we worked hard to execute our strategy to build superior R&D. We were able to create Wyeth's vaunted "class of 2000" new-product flow. We did not secure approval in 2000 for all the new products that we'd hoped for, but during this period Wyeth saw billion-dollar-plus blockbusters emerge from R&D, including Enbrel (for rheumatoid arthritis), Effexor XR (an antidepressant), Prevnar (a vaccine for ear infections) and Protonix (for heartburn). The pharmaceutical industry has long and uncertain lead times for new products—so I was already at PNU when some of these blockbusters hit the market. But I feel proud to this day about how Wyeth changed from a not-very-serious pharmaceutical R&D player in the late 1980s to an industry-leading R&D producer only a decade later. Now that Wyeth is part of Pfizer, it is interesting that the same Prevnar and Enbrel from Wyeth have emerged among Pfizer's bestselling products, particularly after the blockbuster anti-cholesterol product, Lipitor, became genericized in November 2011.

A big reinvention for me came in the form of deal flow at Wyeth. Jack Stafford excelled at the art of deal making, and I learned a lot from him. I worked as part of his small senior team on several deals—and was charged with integrating many of them. Wyeth's acquisitions of other companies flowed at an amazing pace: Robins in 1989, Genetics Institute in 1992 and American Cyanamid/Immunex in 1994. At Wyeth, I again saw how attitude, behavior and culture can produce the decisive advantage.

In the winter of 1997, when CEO recruiter Tom Neff approached me about an interesting public-company CEO job, I had a feeling similar to the one I had when I was approached for the Wyeth job eight years earlier. Like Dr. Moret at Sandoz, Jack Stafford had made me feel valued at Wyeth. I had progressed from being head of Wyeth Domestic to being given the additional responsibilities of R&D, International and the Animal Health and Device businesses. I had rounded off my experience of all Wyeth businesses by being given a rotational assignment to oversee the large American Cyanamid agricultural division after we bought American Cyanamid in 1994. In 1995 Jack had moved me up to executive vice-president and a member of the board of directors. I was being talked about as his eventual replacement.

Yet I *had* to listen to the opportunity being presented. After all, I had succeeded in reinventing myself and my environment at Wyeth. Now, in taking on the adventure of becoming the CEO of Pharmacia & Upjohn (PNU) (a well-publicized and failing merger) and moving to the world headquarters in Europe, I was being presented with yet another reinvention opportunity. I am glad I took that plunge because I went on to reinvent myself *and* my environment as CEO of PNU, and then as CEO of PHA in 2000 and CEO of SGP in 2003.

Toward the end of my reinvention experience at PHA, I was on cruise control during the nine-month wait for regulatory clearances following the July 2002 announcement of the massive ($62 billion) Pharmacia/Pfizer merger. So when I was approached about yet another adventure, my desire to again reinvent myself and my environment made me listen. My subsequent experiences as CEO of Schering-Plough (SGP) actually became the most profound story of turnaround and transformation in my career because the starting point was so difficult.

Life offers endless reinvention opportunities. It is up to us to go for those that match our aspirations.

Chapter Two Takeaway

Be purposeful by having clear goals, venturing out, building energy and renewing yourself periodically.

Chapter 3   Be Connected

The third change-leadership takeaway is to *be connected*, which moves beyond being connected with yourself to being connected with people around you and with your environment.

Part One	Part Two
Be authentic	Keep leading
Be purposeful	Role model your expectations
Be connected	Keep winning

CONNECT AND ALIGN

Stockholm is a beautiful, clean city, untouched by either of the twentieth-century wars in Europe. Its many islands are connected by bridges that span the sparkling waters of the Baltic inlet, known as the Stockholm archipelago. During the long summer evenings, there's no better place in all of Europe to stroll than in the Östermalm neighborhood with its inviting cafés.

Stockholm seemed anything but peaceful to me on one particular morning in June 1997 as I was riding up a delivery elevator at the Cirkus Arena, a magnificent structure built in 1892. It still hosts the circus when it comes to town, but the building is also a multipurpose venue for concerts, exhibitions and, in this case, a rowdy shareholders' meeting. I was about to face hundreds of angry shareholders at the annual meeting of Pharmacia & Upjohn (PNU).

I was experiencing an unnatural level of discomfort. I had just been hired at PNU, taking up the reins after a prolonged leadership vacuum and resultant infighting and politicking. Almost every rock I was turning over had a snake beneath it. Some of the "snakes under the rocks" had bizarre undertones. A senior R&D person (an American) showed me photographs of a family that had been gunned down, mafia style, with the headline "Muerta" on top. He told me the newspaper clipping was slipped under his hotel door in Milan, and that he thought he knew the senior Italian executive who had done it. He warned me to watch out for my own safety. Another top management team executive told me that after every telephone conversation, he heard a distinct click moments after the other party hung up, suggesting his phone was being tapped by the local security head "who belonged to the other side." He too warned me to be careful. I had never seen such a vicious tribal war inside a company!

Public perception wasn't too rosy either. Wall Street was becoming disillusioned as the media ran almost exclusively negative stories about PNU, including anecdotes in the *Wall Street Journal* and *New York Times* about Swedes disappearing for all of July; Italians vanishing for all of August; "insensitive" Americans complaining about the smoking habits of their Italian colleagues; and Italians and Swedes objecting to drug and alcohol testing.

On that June morning in 1997, it really did feel like a circus. Swedish Pharmacia had once been a showpiece company for the country, with tens of thousands of Swedish shareholders. Now, hundreds of them showed up to protest. They expressed their anger at the "Americanization" of their beloved Pharmacia in Swedish; they were also angry at the financial performance of the merged PNU company and at the departing compensation package of the ex-CEO, John Zabriskie, who had been gone since the previous January. I had only been CEO a few weeks, but I wasn't excused from criticism. Some felt that since I was working for a "Swedish" company, I should be paid like a Swedish CEO, and not as the CEO of a Delaware-registered company that was now PNU.

"Why don't you give up your package, Mr. Hassan?" asked one speaker who took the floor, and the crowd cheered at the question. "Why can't we sell products to Cuba?" asked another. The crowd cheered even louder. The board had chosen me because they thought I could reestablish trust where it had been broken, and now I had to start earning it—fast!

Although English is widely understood in Sweden, I spoke slowly so the audience could follow me. I acknowledged their many disappointments. I told them we would develop a plan to salvage the failing merger and turn around the company. I told them I couldn't do much about the differences in compensation systems between Swedish and American CEOs, but that I was asking for their support to help me deal with this dire situation.

Candor builds trust. The audience was frank in their anger. I was frank in my response and in my confidence that the situation could be stabilized and turned around. I left the Cirkus arena feeling that I had established a bond not only with the shareholders assembled there, but also with other Swedish citizens who would be reading about this new CEO who showed up to face the anger.

The experience served me well a few years later when I faced another group of angry shareholders, this time at the Waldorf Astoria hotel in Manhattan, after we announced the Monsanto/PNU merger on December 19, 1999. Earlier, people bought Monsanto stock expecting the previously announced premium deal with Wyeth to go through. It had fallen apart. Now, they would be getting far less than they had hoped for. Although the anger was almost entirely directed at the Monsanto management, as the designated CEO of the proposed newly merged company, Pharmacia (PHA), I had to work on taming it. It took patience, listening, empathizing and telling the story of what we had in mind to bring back the trust—and we did. We re-recruited the people who were angry. The merger closed three months later with no interlopers showing up, despite the low premium for Monsanto.

It is unusual to twice take over a large public company as CEO and face angry shareholders just before the annual shareholders' meeting without being introduced by my predecessor. On April 22, 2003, Schering-Plough's annual meeting was held less than 72 hours after my first day as CEO. Not unlike the PNU situation six years earlier, the press had been reporting very negatively on the company's fall from grace. Emotions were running high. So high, in fact, that the security department insisted on installing a metal detector and bulletproof furniture, and on hiring a crowd-control specialist. Full praise should go to every member of the Schering-Plough board who had the courage to sit on the stage and face the crowd that morning at the Sheraton Hotel in Iselin, New Jersey.

The nastiness at the SGP annual meeting was similar to what I had experienced six years earlier at the Cirkus Arena in Stockholm. When it was my turn to speak, I think my reputation as a tested CEO at both PNU and PHA helped me. I told the audience frankly that I had alternatives, but SGP was the challenge that motivated me the most. I shared with them the transformation road as visualized in my Playbook Gantt chart (Figure 3.1). I told them that this stepping-stone approach had repeatedly worked for me in the past, and that with their patience and support, I believed the company could be brought to strength.[1]

---

[1] This Gantt chart is explained in more detail in Appendix F.

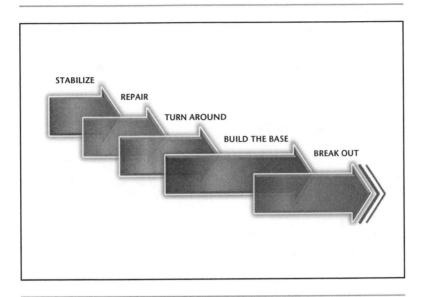

FIGURE 3.1   The Playbook Gantt Chart

As in Stockholm, I believe that candor and confidence helped me build trust at this SGP annual meeting. At the end of the meeting, though, no one was more relieved than the security staff.

Connecting and aligning with internal stakeholders is as important as with external stakeholders. When people's careers and livelihoods are on the line, they seek to develop an extra special connection with the CEO and the Team at the Top. But a pre-requisite for this is that the CEO and his Level 2s must act with integrity and authenticity so that they can rapidly earn the trust of the people they lead.

One example of connecting and aligning was my personal signing of our Consent Decree as the incoming Schering Plough CEO. This decree, which was unprecedented in scope, had preceded my arrival by a few months. It encompassed extensive manufacturing and R&D obligations. I took on this additional personal risk because I felt a sense of duty to help get the company "out of jail." In September 2007, four years later, we had an emotional celebration in our cafeteria. This massive Consent Decree had not only been lifted by the FDA—and with not one additional enforcement action—we also had earned trust with the FDA and made major advances toward building a culture of integrity in all parts of the company.

When going into a volatile situation, it is important for the new leader to connect and align with the stakeholders—even when he or she doesn't have the answers.

TAKE EARLY ACTION STEPS

When I arrived at Schering-Plough in April 2003, I did what I had done previously upon taking charge of an organization. One of my very first tasks was to have each of the company's vice-presidents take a written survey, without having to reveal their names or job responsibilities. They were asked open-ended questions, such as, "What are the priorities that need immediate attention?" "What would you do if you were the CEO?" "What are the barriers that prevent you from doing your job, and do you have any suggestions regarding how to remove them?" "Do you have any other comments?"

After the answers were submitted, a third party analyzed them. The results were clear. As had been the case when I arrived at PNU, the vice-presidents revealed high levels of dismay and feelings of being victims. And this was among vice-presidents—the very group to whom others looked up to lead the company!

I shared the essence of the feedback with the vice-presidents, the board members and the rest of the company. The data convinced the people at SGP that they were *ready* for change.

When asking our Schering-Plough colleagues to make sacrifices, I worked hard to paint a picture of the improvements that would be made as we advanced along our six- to eight-year action agenda. We envisioned a more diverse product portfolio with a stronger exclusivity profile, a richer R&D pipeline, higher employee-engagement scores, rising sales and improving margins. We published a core document that was an inspirational read, rather than the usual book of rules. The document helped us motivate our employees to put in a sustained positive attitude and hard work.

We worked hard to make Schering-Plough colleagues understand that the work they did was important to our shared vision—and that each of them could *make a difference* and *facilitate positive change*.

We explained that to execute our business missions, we preferred winning teams to rock stars. We discussed that even though SGP was under-resourced and smaller than its biggest Big Pharma competitors, we could, together, do extraordinary things. We noted that throughout history, organizations with the "will to win" have often outperformed much bigger and better-resourced rivals.

During my first 200 days at SGP, I laid the groundwork for change by dividing my time among the following four groups:

- senior and middle managers
- frontline managers
- customers
- authorities and lawmakers

Interaction with these four groups was invaluable, and it allowed me to move forward with confidence and speed. Six months after taking charge, I knew I had succeeded in getting their buy-in.

This Playbook puts a high premium on early wins as a way to start building credibility and change momentum. At the same time, it is important to show restraint on many big actions until the game-changing moves become clearer.

"*When* are we going to see some big changes?" I have been probed more than once with this type of question during the early months of my various CEO and general-management assignments. Doing less in the first 200 days than in the following 200 may defy conventional wisdom. However, this initial period is crucial to connecting and building credibility. It is the time to focus on listening, learning, tuning in and planning. Doing this well lays the groundwork for the purposeful and relentless change that follows. "Go slow to go fast" is the mantra for this part of my Playbook. "Go slow" is not an option in all cases. At both SGP (which was burning about $1 billion of cash annually) and PNU (which was in an alarming downward spiral caused by internal tribalism), the initial

Stabilize and Repair stages of the Playbook Gantt chart required some quick and decisive actions—often based on gut instincts.

Business metrics *follow* attitude, behavior and culture (ABC). A strong culture improves productivity because team spirit becomes second nature and people help each other while also building on each other's work. Sales growth, profit growth and earnings-per-share growth are among the lagging indicators that come from the leading indicators of good people, good strategies, good action plans, a good culture and good organizational health.

Any change leader's first task is to convince people that they are ready for change. Then the leader builds credibility by acting and following through in a deliberate, decisive and consistent manner.

VALUE EQ AS MUCH AS IQ

We've all heard of IQ (intelligence quotient). But IQ doesn't measure strong leadership qualities such as insight, self-awareness, creativity, empathy, common sense, connectivity, integrity and sense of humor. These qualities define "emotional quotient" or EQ. I've worked with both brilliant individuals who were not effective leaders because they lacked emotional intelligence, and individuals whose high emotional quotient (EQ) enabled them to become effective leaders beyond what their grade point average might have suggested.

It may be helpful to differentiate between experience and EQ. Experience comes from knowledge, insights and learning from failures and successes. Experience gives us the power of gut instinct to make good moves even when we don't have enough time or data to do full analyses, or when we face many unknowns. A high IQ clearly improves one's experience, but high EQ improves it to an even greater degree.

Annie McKee, one of the founders of the Teleos Leadership Institute, applies the concept of emotional intelligence to corporate leadership. McKee writes, "By 2006, not only had [Schering-Plough] sustained double-digit growth for several consecutive quarters, but it had also outperformed all its competitors on critical organizational climate dimensions. In virtually all categories, scores on vital aspects of climate and morale were higher by an unprecedented margin."[2]

I use various terms to describe high-EQ behaviors in different situations. High Leadership EQ means demonstrating high EQ as a leader. High Social EQ, Team EQ, Board EQ, Partnering EQ, M&A EQ, Matrix EQ and Fiscal EQ are terms I use to describe high-EQ behaviors when people are in specific situations. Even though these are not widely used terms, people tune in very quickly to what I am saying.

Why is it important for you as a manager or aspiring manager to have a high EQ? Because your attitude and behavior have an enormous impact on those you work with and, especially, on those you supervise. In fact, emotional intelligence becomes even more important than functional knowledge and skills as you progress up the corporate ladder and begin to manage managers. At the CEO level, a high EQ is critical to the CEO's ability to leverage the ABC Advantage.

A leader's success with emotional intelligence is also manifested in how his teams behave (Team EQ), especially during times of stress or opportunity. A high Team EQ becomes a powerful enhancer of the team's performance when team members are in tune with each other, respect each other's positions and can count on each other.

The CEO helps build Team EQ by assembling and developing a team of A-players. An A-player, for instance, is someone who not only performs her delegated job and *excels* at doing it, but also *understands* her colleagues' work and *connects* with them easily. If the leader has senior-level A-players who rise to the occasion and who provide complete support when asked to work as a team with a boundaryless attitude, then that leader can delegate to *that* team with trust. As CEO, I was able to go on vacations or distant-country visits with the knowledge that my team had the professional excellence and the high Team EQ to keep the company in good shape in my absence.

---

[2] Annie McKee, Richard E. Boyatzis, and Fran Johnston, *Becoming a Resonant Leader: Develop Your Emotional Intelligence, Renew Your Relationships, Sustain Your Effectiveness* (Boston: Harvard Business Press, 2008).

A high EQ drives good mentoring. Two-way conversations between supervisor and employee can lead to productive coaching and mentoring for not only the employee but also the supervisor. Similarly, older managers can be "reverse mentored" by their younger direct or indirect reports. The pace of change from the baby boomer generation, to Generation X, to the Millennials/Generation Y is so huge that this reverse mentoring—especially in digital technologies and new media—can yield huge benefits. As I moved up the senior ladder at a young age, I ended up having people who were much older than I was reporting to me. This is one of those situations in which high Leadership EQ is really necessary. Older people need to be treated with sensitivity and respect for their experience and wisdom. I have often succeeded in co-opting the older executives to join my inner team—and I benefited a lot as a result. An older person in such a situation also needs a high Team EQ to know that his younger boss has her job to do, and that the younger boss needs his positive attitude and support. An older manager can still find work to be fulfilling if he can develop trust and a good interpersonal contract with his new boss.

Emotional intelligence can also come into play when you're off the clock. During the 1980s, I had a direct report who was flying back from Puerto Rico to New Jersey with my boss. I heard later that he watched a movie instead of using the time to get to know my boss better. In this case, the employee's low Social EQ was part of other behaviors that failed to build trust, and he ended up leaving the company.

President Clinton is perhaps the best-known example of someone with a high Social EQ (even though he had other EQ failures). I was seated next to him at a dinner in Washington, DC, in 1999—and also at a charity function in New York City a few years later. He makes you feel that he understands you. He responds in a manner that shows that he respects what you have to say—even if he may not actually agree with you.

In general, to exemplify a high Social EQ, one should use common sense and sensitivity in social interactions, in giving appropriate feedback or praise and in respectfully disagreeing with a colleague, a direct report or even a supervisor. Be aware of good business etiquette—whether it's in dress, salutations, wining and dining or sending a thoughtful note. I know a mega-company CEO, who was subsequently fired, who at CEO gatherings would keep glancing through the sides of his eyes while he was talking to you, looking for a more "important" conversation. I also know a Level 2 executive who, after being hired, found the private addresses of each board member and sent them all personal notes. Obviously, this did not exemplify high Social EQ, since none of the board members had either given him their addresses or invited the contact. Business etiquette, as we understand it in the United States, may not necessarily "travel" to other countries, so one must be aware of local mores and cultures.

Another major "EQ derailer" is when aspiring managers wear their ambitions on their sleeve, always looking for the next power position in the organizational chart. They do not build trust because their self-centered agenda compromises team building. I have seen many smart, hardworking people whose self-centered behaviors derailed their once-promising careers.

Throughout my own career, I have always taken pride in working hard on what is in front of me, not focusing on the next raise or looking around for political opportunities. The responsibilities, the raises and the recognition have always come. Building trust with one's colleagues and one's supervisor is key.

High-EQ leaders have the self-confidence and poise to keep themselves from taking disagreements or someone else's deficit in manners as a personal affront. They are more sensitive to others, more flexible, more emotionally resilient—and, most importantly, better equipped to spring back from difficult challenges.

It is natural for leaders to occasionally show their emotions or even pound the table. However, continuous domineering or overbearing behavior is bad for the supervisor's health and, even worse, for the health of those being supervised. One should avoid being such a boss or working for such a boss. Cortisol, the stress hormone, is part of what makes up our ambitious nature. High EQ habits should enable us to channel it into constructive activities, like vigorous physical workouts or self-education, as opposed to taking it out on those whom we supervise—and putting our own health at risk. I have seen many domineering managers become shooting stars—they flame out. Few supporters show up for them when they start to fall.

The self-awareness and self-control that derive from a high EQ will enable you to remain flexible and mature in your reasoning as you make plans and execute them. Understand the upsides and the downsides of your action plan. When the execution is not on plan, ask yourself, is it the changed environment? Is it the plan? Is it my execution? What should I change?

Once you've answered these kinds of questions, take action. Make changes. There is tremendous learning and excitement as we meet life's unexpected challenges. By doing something about them, we feel liberated and empowered.

Finally, there is a life-enhancement aspect to emotional intelligence. We all know that money doesn't necessarily make us rich inside. Richness comes from having a positive attitude, from acting with purpose, from having a social system—and playing a meaningful role in it. High EQ is not only a leadership enabler, but also a great way to make life more purposeful.

Valuing high EQ and leading with a high EQ builds strength.

RESPECT YOUR BOSS'S POSITION

In our careers, we all get bosses who do not rise to our expectations. Some can be domineering; others can create confusion and wasted motion with frequent changes in strategies or priorities. Still others can be so insecure that they don't take a stand when they should. Each case needs a careful and customized approach. If a boss doesn't think you are on her side, she can become passive-aggressive and find ways to derail your career. I have found that earning the trust of one's imperfect boss rather than being judgmental about her shortcomings is much more productive.

In the 1970s, I had a boss who would not ask for help from headquarters—because *his* immediate boss was very political, and my boss would feel embarrassed if he requested help. Fortunately, the global division head from headquarters, while visiting the site where I worked, asked for a one-on-one with me. During our conversation, I found a way to educate this senior decision maker about what we needed—free patient starter samples for doctors for a new product launch. We received the samples, the launch was successful and my boss got the credit. I built trust with him in the process.

Building trust with and respecting one's supervisor improves productivity.

TUNE IN

Tuning in is a powerful way to demonstrate one's high EQ. Tuning in means listening, relating and empathizing. It means being in touch with people and with one's environment. Leaders who excel at this become good at not only seeing around corners but also at seeing all the way to the horizon—and beyond. Being in tune is more than simply *saying* that we empathize with and relate to people. It means really tuning in, as we would tune in to a radio frequency. It means creating teams where all members are tuned in to how well they are accomplishing their assigned tasks.

Tuning in greatly helped me to become stronger as a leader. For example, when taking charge of a stressful situation, I often included in my team people who I already knew, especially when there would be no second chance and when time was at a premium. It reduced the hiring risk and the time it would take to adjust to each others' styles and expectations. However, I always made sure these new hires were A-players who would gain instant credibility. For instance, in my early days at Schering-Plough, I brought in Bob Bertolini as CFO and Tom Sabatino as chief legal officer. I had met, benchmarked and validated both of these executives at an earlier time—and now I knew I could trust them and that they would command instant credibility. They did!

It is essential to identify *early* who among the various operating teams in the company are the key drivers and the opinion leaders. Establishing powerful trusting relationships with these individuals and encouraging good relationships among them is especially important in getting tuned in. By developing a network of influential boosters, it is easier to execute the change agenda.

After getting in tune with the inside of the organization, you need to get in tune with the outside. Tune in to how competitors will act and react. It is also very important to tune in to the larger ecosystem—especially as one goes up the ladder. As one approaches the C-suite, understanding the broader insights of civics, macroeconomics, political science and the interaction of the public and private sectors becomes more and more important.

When taking over a company in distress, get in tune with your most important stakeholders: customers, investors, company colleagues and other people who matter. Ask them to give you the time you need to fix what's broken. Understand your environment and how it will change. Tune in to the customers and try to sense what will satisfy or even delight them. Good customer analytics are a basic tool, but having a genuine empathy for customers helps a lot more with tuning in. Tuning in, in this context, also means sensing evolving technologies and the evolving moves of competitors, and anticipating the expectations of other stakeholders—including the authorities and investors.

Once we are in tune, we are ready to execute with excellence. Executional excellence includes internalizing the strategy, then planning, aligning, organizing, energizing and relentlessly following through. It also includes tracking progress and making adjustments. (Also see Chapter Six.)

After you've tuned in, it is important to *stay* in tune. For example, once a company is on the road to recovery, it is natural for everyone on the team to take a deep, well-deserved breath. But one must fight the "complacency creep" syndrome. "We're now doing okay" is not good enough. As the wins occur, companies and people need to recharge their commitment. The Executional Excellence Spiral requires an attitude of dedication and resilience to keep making "better" even better.

Begin by getting in tune with yourself, with your people and with your environment. Help your people to be in tune with each other.

Make certain that everyone knows what is expected of them as individuals and what to expect of each other as teammates. Inspire your people to follow you.

PRACTICE ACTIVE LISTENING

Active listening helps you to better understand the message. In some cases it allows you to understand and also to *do* something with that understanding.

I was having lunch with my friend Mike Evanisko in my Wyeth office in Radnor, Pennsylvania, in November of 1992 when I said, "Mike, almost half of all our efforts to treat patients with our medicines go to waste because half of the patients do not stay with their chronic meds six months after their initial prescription." Mike listened. He understood and then he *did* something about it. He started a company called Adheris, which helped patients stay on their medicines. Everybody won. Patients benefited from better health. The pharmaceutical companies did more business, pharmacies filled more prescriptions and the health-care system saved money because pharmaceuticals are highly cost-effective. Adheris did so well that ultimately another company paid over $100 million for it.

Insatiable curiosity will make you feel enriched, never bored and younger than your biological age. The relentless desire to actively listen, learn, observe, gain insights and connect the dots helps to advance our knowledge, skills and creativity.

We must listen to and learn from stakeholders, competitors and especially colleagues. It's amazing what can be accomplished by simply *asking* people, especially frontline managers, for their opinions. How many smart people are poor listeners and end up being surprised at their results? At the same time, being a good listener does not mean doing what the last person you talked to recommends, or compromising your values and beliefs. My grandmother taught me to "listen to all, but in the end follow your own instincts."

It's one thing to listen; it's another thing to actually understand what is said. Data has to be turned into information, then it has to be turned into knowledge. Knowledge is only useful after thinking and understanding. If a piece of knowledge is important, repeat what you've just heard—to yourself and to those who have told it to you. If it's worth remembering, write it down if possible. That will not only help you remember it but also demonstrate that you are listening, encouraging more feedback.

Sometimes you have to listen to meanings beyond the words. By feeding back your understanding of the conversation, the person with whom you are speaking can either confirm or correct your understanding. Additionally, train yourself to sharpen your learning through visual observations of and cues from the other person. These are simple tools that will greatly improve your strategic insights—insights that become a critical aspect of leadership as one goes from Level 3 to Level 2 to Level 1. Especially at Level 1, strategic insights are crucial and the appetite for learning needs to be large. I often get asked why I bother to learn so much when I can rely on people around me. My answer is that if I know more, I can understand better. People get energized when they feel their leader is committed to knowing more about the business and has a hunger to learn.

Inside the organization, listening and tuning in includes connecting the dots *among* the functions. R&D discovers new products. Marketing and sales deal with product, place, promotion, price and sales interactions. Supply chain oversees purchasing, manufacturing and logistics. The above three key functions are woven together by global functions such as human resources (people), legal (laws and contracts) and accounting (the common numerical vocabulary for business activities and results). While managers can do a good job coordinating *between* the functions, good leaders create emotional energy and positive interactions *among* the functions as a convergent team.

Strong listening skills are foundational for serially successful leaders.

BUILD INFORMATION FLUIDITY

Ever wonder why the United States leads Europe in innovation in biosciences? In the United States, there is better information fluidity among academia, the National Institutes of Health (NIH) and the private sector. When there is information fluidity, active listening and learning become easier.

In October 2009, during Cleveland Clinic's annual Medical Innovation Summit, journalist and news anchor Maria Bartiromo interviewed me as a keynote guest in front of an audience of academic, business and medical leaders. As Bartiromo opened the floor to questions, I realized that the people present did not care whether one was from the for-profit or the not-for-profit sector. They cared only to share knowledge and to celebrate medical advances. This annual event demonstrates how important information fluidity is in creating major competitive advantages.

Leaders should encourage and expect information fluidity. In the spring of 1976, as I moved up the ranks at Dorsey Laboratories, I decided to confront the vertical and horizontal silos that often hold back productivity in organizations. At a sales and marketing managers' meeting in Jacksonville, Florida, I was more assertive than usual. I felt I needed to be brutally honest. I advised the managers to exude "no nonsense on business matters, but to move freely and easily among the people." I told them that I expected them to be empathetic and friendly to colleagues at all levels of the company, but at the same time to always expect business excellence. I reminded them that easy interaction among all colleagues fosters information fluidity.

At a follow-up meeting, I handed out "Sales and Marketing" T-shirts to illustrate that there should be no gap between the two functions. Information fluidity improved dramatically in the following four years, which led to such an unusually strong sales and marketing culture at Dorsey that when the internal merger between it and the much larger Sandoz occurred in 1980, the Dorsey people tended to emerge on top.

Strive to build information fluidity inside you and around you.

BUILD PARTNERING SKILLS

Partnering is the "new normal" in the twenty-first century. Companies partner in order to pool resources, reduce overheads and share risk. In Japan, beginning in the 1930s, Toyota demonstrated that it understood early the importance of *nurturing* a network of supply-chain partners.

In the summer of 1997, only a few weeks after accepting the CEO position at the ailing Pharmacia & Upjohn (PNU), I was with frontline managers in Uppsala, Sweden, when I first learned that one of our major hopes in the R&D pipeline had already been compromised by a junior manager in the previously "decentralized" Swedish company, Pharmacia. Forest Labs, a company headquartered in New York City, would be claiming rights in the U.S. market to Detrol, PNU's late-stage R&D product for overactive bladder.

A few weeks later, many of us were sweating as we attended the arbitration hearings before three judges in London. Howard Solomon, CEO of Forest Labs, had brought some heavy guns to testify for them.

My relationship with Howard Solomon went back to the 1980s. My company, Sandoz, had partnered with Forest Labs to leverage its special drug-delivery technology. I used my trust card with Howard. He knew my back was against the wall, and that I was not going to let go of Detrol. Over an October weekend in 1997, before the arbitrators came back with their decision, we cut a deal. PNU would buy the U.S. rights to Detrol for $25 million. This payment to Forest was huge for an already stressed PNU, but Detrol—after FDA approval—became a billion-dollar blockbuster.

Often a personal outreach can gain an advantage over otherwise stronger competition. When, in October 2001, Pharmacia was looking to in-license Daxas, a lung disease product (whose novelty lay in the fact that it was orally administered instead of inhaled), from a German company called Altana, I was able to pick up the phone and call their pharmaceutical division CEO in Germany. He told me that we were late to the party, and that there were larger companies ahead of us. But the fact that I was the only Big Pharma CEO who personally called him made the difference. He let us in, and we ended up being selected as Altana's partner.

A broader definition of partnering includes outsourcing— another accelerating trend of the twenty-first century. It is surprising how frequently one hears from outsourcing companies that they appreciate the business—but their counterparts at their "large company" partner fail to get the best work from them because there is either arrogance or ignorance about how to be a good partner.

At Schering-Plough, we were early pioneers in inviting outsourcing partners to become embedded *in* the company. This approach worked especially well in R&D. R&D in Big Pharma needs to reduce its fixed-cost structure in order to increase its flexibility to be opportunistic with expensive clinical trials when promising product leads show up.

High Partnering EQ—which is based on the trust that develops between parties—becomes the catalyst that enables two disparate cultures to win together. Success should be measured not only by what partnerships accomplish in ordinary times, but especially by what they accomplish in times of stress or opportunity.

PLUG INTO THE POWER GRID

Working in a complex Swiss corporation for 17 years helped me build strength by becoming a good matrix player. The matrix structure has been around for 80 years, but making the matrix work remains a challenge at many large companies. A *matrix player* is someone who effectively works through persuasion and influence—without needing to resort to formal positional power on the organization chart. She works with other departments, has the ability to obtain data and information in a seamless manner without exerting a big toll on the organization and persuades people in other departments as a matrix leader. *She treats a large global organization as a power grid and has the ability to plug into it, both absorbing and feeding into its power.*

Everyone can be a leader, even if one is not in a traditional positional leadership role. Everyone can also have a high Leadership EQ or Matrix EQ that allows one to be a strong *team player* when someone else—even outside the department or at a lower level on the organizational chart—takes the lead.

Plugging into the *outside* power grid is another way to build strength. In early 1995 I was on a helicopter flight from northern

New Jersey to Pennsylvania. With me was Dr. Leon Smith, a world expert in infectious diseases. Leon had made the time for this trip because he and I had a relationship going back to my days at Sandoz. His candor had earned my trust, and at times I took his advice to avoid certain projects. On this day, we were visiting the Wyeth pharmaceutical team in Pennsylvania to determine the fate of Zosyn, a product for hospital infections that had landed in Wyeth's hands after its acquisition of American Cyanamid in November 1994. Zosyn had struggled since its FDA approval in the United States in November 1993, and sentiment was building within the post-acquisition team to put our resources elsewhere. On the helicopter ride back to New Jersey, Dr. Smith was candid—as he had been in the past. "This one is a winner," he told me. "Just don't let it get ruined because it is part of an acquired company." I followed Dr. Smith's advice, and Zosyn ultimately became a billion-dollar blockbuster. Plugging into the *outside* power grid worked!

A few years later, at PNU, I asked Dr. Smith about Zyvox, another hospital anti-infective. This R&D-stage product was at risk of falling through the cracks in the wake of the failing PNU merger. Dr. Smith told me that resistance to hospital infections was rising, and since Zyvox was a powerful compound from a new class, the deadly bacteria would be more vulnerable and build less resistance to it. As a result, I, along with Goran Ando (the head of R&D), championed Zyvox with the research team in Kalamazoo, Michigan. It took another $300 million in R&D costs, but Zyvox did get approved by the FDA in April 2000. In 2010 it reached $1.2 billion in sales and, more importantly, of course, has saved many, many lives.

Plugging into the power grid builds strength for the individual and the team.

GROW EVERY SECTOR OF LIFE

Sandoz U.S. was having a Thanksgiving celebration in November 1987 at the Skylands banquet hall in Randolph, New Jersey. This was also a time to say thanks for the strong progress on our transformation road and to ask for renewed determination going forward. Following the crucial turnaround in late 1984, we had maintained a high-energy environment for three consecutive years, and the company had finished another year of strong double-digit growth (both top and bottom line).

Almost everyone from our New Jersey site, whether in office jobs, in the labs or in the factory, was gathered with his or her spouse or partner. The orchestra kept the people dancing. I wanted people to believe in themselves and to taste victory. I also wanted people to understand that we were in it together, from Level 1 through Level 8.

Mixing among so many levels and having fun together was a culture shock for many. Big Pharma didn't do things like that! This kind of mixing was reserved for the cash-hungry biotechs! I surprised the group further when I talked in my speech about growing in all dimensions, including work, home, community and self. I told them that the latter was the easiest to neglect. I also shared with them my own goal to invest at least one hour a week in some self-improvement—and to try to break a sweat before noon, through exercise, at least five times a week. The message resonated with the audience, although, like me, many knew that "balance" is an impossible ideal. There have to be trade-offs—but I really meant it when I told the audience that we should try to grow a bit in each of the four dimensions.

I made my trade-offs. As I got busier at work, I drastically lightened up on activities such as golf to make time for what was most important to me. My weekends continued to be devoted to family time and high-volume reading and paperwork. My positive attitude toward work made the trade-off easy.

My home life has been enriched by my wife and best friend of 43 years, Noreen, and our three children and two grandchildren. A tight-knit family and a close connection with our extended family, our friends and the charities we support have been sources of inner strength for me.

Grow every sector of your life and make the trade-offs if you need to excel at something.

Chapter Three Takeaway

Listen to yourself, tune in to people and plug into your environment.

■ ■ ■

Chapters One, Two and Three are about becoming stronger and making people around you stronger. Here, in summary, are the change-leadership takeaways from these chapters.

Part One	
Be authentic	**Value integrity.** **Know who you are.** **Know what you want to do with your life and career.**
Be purposeful	**Have clear goals.** **Venture out and build energy.** **Renew yourself periodically.**
Be connected	**Listen to yourself.** **Tune in to people.** **Plug into your environment.**

Two

UNLEASHING THE POWER OF *WE*

How to Make the Organization Stronger

Part One of this book talked about the *me* part of my Playbook. It focused on making you and the people around you stronger. Part Two will cover the *we* part, and will focus on making the team as a whole stronger. As mentioned in the Introduction, many of the attitudes and behaviors discussed in Part One also apply to Part Two. The three major change-leadership takeaways of Part Two are: *keep leading, role model your expectations* and *keep winning.*

Chapter Four covers the first change-leadership takeaway: *keep leading*. The chapter focuses on picking good people, and aligning and motivating them.

The second change-leadership takeaway, the subject of Chapter Five, is *role model your expectations* to make the team stronger. This involves inculcating winning behaviors, expecting leaders to lead and building trust.

The final takeaway, as detailed in Chapter Six, is to make the team stronger to keep winning. This includes fostering team trust and alignment, executing for results and driving the virtuous spiral upward.

Chapter 4   Keep Leading

The first change-leadership takeaway in making the team stronger is to *keep leading*. This involves picking good people, and aligning and motivating them.

Part One	Part Two
Be authentic	**Keep leading**
Be purposeful	**Role model your expectations**
Be connected	**Keep winning**

DEVELOP THE POWER TRIANGLE

In January 1984, Sandoz U.S. was in difficult straits. The 1980 internal merger between Sandoz and Dorsey had led to culture clashes, tribalism, executive exits and the poor integration of systems. Sandoz's largest drug, Mellaril (for psychosis), had recently lost its patent exclusivity and was in a downward trajectory as freshly arriving generics eroded its space. The FDA had turned up the heat on the company's manufacturing, quality assurance and compliance practices. The turmoil in the quality operations had also involved, quite sadly, the suicide of a senior manager in that area. The Sandoz U.S. assignment had been without a permanent head for almost a year. There would now be so much urgency and such a penalty for failure in this largest of Sandoz's country operations that my Playbook had to work quickly—and work with my first attempt.

Two weeks after taking charge, I was with the frontline sales managers at a meeting in Rancho Las Palmas in California. By establishing credibility—fast—with this group, we started the Stabilize and Repair part of our action agenda (as outlined in my Playbook Gantt chart). I again made the case for change. Everywhere the message was the same: it didn't matter whether you were former Sandoz or former Dorsey or former somewhere else; as long as you had a positive attitude, professional excellence, energy and team spirit, you were going to do well. We were building a meritocracy.

As I would repeat during later turnarounds, we were developing the Power Triangle of *People*, *Products* and *Processes* as a core pathway to drive culture change and to build value with customers and other outside stakeholders. *People* formed the base of the triangle (Figure 4.1).

At Sandoz U.S., we assembled good people and ensured that they were aligned with the transformation journey. Next, we turned our attention to *Products*. Products are the vehicles for connecting with customers and driving sales and earnings. Products in the Sandoz portfolio, such as Pamelor (an antidepressant), that had been given up as failures suddenly started to blossom. Good *Processes* add to the power of people and products. Processes became better in all

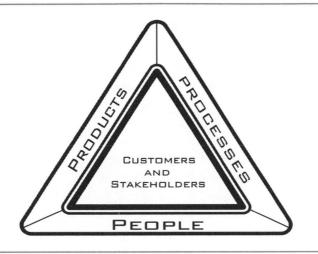

FIGURE 4.1   The Power Triangle
Source: Bausch + Lomb

parts of the business, but especially in sales force effectiveness (SFE), where Tim Rothwell, the newly appointed head of sales operations, engineered a 30-percent increase in sales force productivity. We stunned corporate headquarters in Basel by quickly moving into double-digit top- and bottom-line growth territory— and then staying there year after year. Our convincing turnaround had a huge impact on showing a previously skeptical and dispirited U.S. organization that everybody could not only *own* change, but also be part of *driving* transformational change.

In October 1985, about 3,000 Sandoz colleagues assembled in the Mennen Sports Arena in northern New Jersey on dark-blue carpeting that covered the ice-skating rink. The meeting was the first of its kind in company history, and I had the irrational fear that the ice would melt with the energy and excitement in the arena. The meeting celebrated the company's critical turnaround and closed past merger wounds. The organizing group even developed a stirring company song called "We Share the Spirit, the Sandoz Spirit" to symbolize the new attitude. This attitude looked beyond the turnaround to what would become a transformation journey.

We were going to keep winning together. We were going to take Sandoz into the top 10 pharmaceutical companies in the U.S. and soon zoom through the $1-billion sales threshold.

During the subsequent years, the ongoing cultural transformation continued. People worked on improving themselves, their colleagues and their productivity as a team. We continued to have strong double-digit growth every year until my departure in 1989 to Wyeth. Today, I note with pride that Sandoz's successor company, Novartis, continues to be a successful mega-company with a strong culture. Dan Vasella, who joined our Sandoz U.S. commercial team as a practicing physician from Bern, Switzerland, has been instrumental as a change-agent CEO at Novartis (realizing $51 billion in annual sales in 2010). In October 2006, the *Financial Times* quoted Dan as saying that I was his early mentor. I am proud to see his success as an inspirational leader of Novartis, and of pharmaceutical innovation with breakthroughs like the anti-cancer medication Gleevec.

Working effectively on the right combination of People, Products and Processes delivers value to customers and other stakeholders.

PUT PEOPLE FIRST

Once one gets the People part right, the strategies around Products and Processes become much easier. Choosing A-players at Levels 2 and 3 is critical in making certain that the senior team provides strong leadership to the rest. A-players attract A-players, Bs attract Bs and Cs. The key to the People part of the Power Triangle is to attract, retain, develop, engage and motivate competent people who also have the *attitude* to win. A-players, working as individuals and in teams, focus on doing the right things and doing them well. They have the *professional excellence* to remain cutting-edge and proactive, the *energy* to work hard and the *team spirit* to build energy around them. You gain people's commitment by helping them to develop a powerful sense of purpose—and by reinforcing the belief among them that *they matter in getting things done.*

No matter how large the company, the CEO has to see himself as the chief people leader. As CEO, I made it part of my duties to remain visible to my people in big and small meetings, and also to build and keep rejuvenated the best "people funnel" possible. Our head of HR always served as my chief partner in this. This funnel supplied A-players, both from inside and outside the organization.

Nurturing the people funnel is important. For high-potential employees (high-potentials), we tried to create development scenarios for them, including developmental rotations. In many cases, we left them where they were, but attempted to expand their assignments so they would be challenged and tested. I am proud of our huge worldwide alumni base of A-players who continue to excel in their careers.

In 2000, when we merged Pharmacia & Upjohn with Monsanto to create Pharmacia, a company with about 60,000 employees worldwide, I made it my business to get to know the company's top 200 managers personally. I don't mean the top 200 according to hierarchy, but rather the top 200 according to potential and the degree to which they contributed to company goals. I, along with the head of HR, tried to get to know them, identified their strengths and weaknesses, and monitored their progress.

My attention did not end only with the high-potentials. I also interacted with the frontlines to observe strong people who might be candidates for the senior leadership in 10 to 20 years. When I went to a sales meeting, I often sat with frontline sales managers or the highest-performing sales reps chosen by the frontline managers. All of this contact was time-consuming, but it allowed me to remain tuned in.

Organizations need to spend more effort *developing* talent than recruiting talent. Talent management is not the sole responsibility of the CEO or head of the human resources department. It should be practiced at all levels of the organization. For example, line managers should be expected to help their immediate subordinates with their professional development.

Sometimes, of course, a talented executive's appetite for a higher-level job exceeds the company's capacity, and you may have to say, "You have done a good job. We've rewarded you financially. Currently we cannot fulfill your timeline, so you may be happier elsewhere." Losing good people is unfortunate, but as your company becomes a "development factory," you can expect to lose some good executives to rivals. Consider it a validation of your talent-development culture. Besides, this type of turnover opens up new opportunities for other colleagues to stretch themselves.

Make credible people decisions, starting with the Team at the Top. This should help cascade high-quality people decisions at other levels.

ASSESS AND DEVELOP PEOPLE

Recognition and rewards are important. It becomes easier to engage people when you build a strong sense of purpose and a fair recognition-and-reward environment.[1]

While running the global pharmaceutical division at Wyeth in 1993, I looked at the incentive plans of various country operations. I noticed with surprise that all sales reps in Italy were getting the same bonus regardless of who made the most sales. Good leaders motivate the outperformers in their teams with the prospect

---

[1] Part of this discussion originally appeared as an interview in "In Search of Global Leaders," *Harvard Business Review*, August 2003.

of higher recognition and reward. We not only changed that situation, but later we also ensured that our company policies made it clear that we believed in differentiation—not only in base and incentive compensation, but also in separating the high-potentials for more challenges, job rotations and more development. Some companies avoid or curtail individual differentiation, as they feel it hurts team spirit. *Although we emphasized individual differentiation, the criteria for differentiation included the employee's contribution to team spirit and to the company culture.*

Our performance-planning and appraisal systems were used as culture-change tools at all the companies I led. Employees who get regular coaching and feedback from their supervisors have much higher engagement (and consequently better performance) scores than those who don't. At SGP, managers and their people were encouraged to maintain a frequent informal dialogue throughout the year on skill building and performance against objectives as part of our Performance Management Planning (PMP) system.

Our PMP sessions were designed to maximize connectivity between the supervisor and the employee by setting expectations, assessing performance versus objectives, coaching, skill building and discussing compensation. Our PMP system contributed positively to organizational productivity. By giving people the *right* to expect a minimum of three conversations annually, we helped improve their engagement and their productivity (Figure 4.2).

Session 1 (usually in December/January) incorporated the employee's prior-year performance versus objectives. Most importantly, it clarified the employee's business and personal-development objectives for the coming year. Session 2 (usually in February/March) was a compensation discussion that included salary, bonus and stock incentives. Session 3 (usually in June/July) was a midyear performance review, coupled with a coaching and skill-building discussion.

A distinctive feature of the PMP was that the compensation discussion (Session 2) was kept separate from Sessions 1 and 3, so that coaching and skill building occurred without the distraction of compensation issues. The other distinctive feature was the

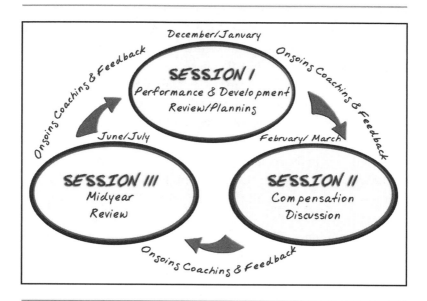

FIGURE 4.2   Schering-Plough's Performance Management Planning Sessions
Source: SGP/Merck

training that we gave to supervisors, which enabled them to give and to expect candid feedback. The latter is usually not done well in conventional performance-assessment systems.

The PMP process was initially developed as a pilot project for Level 2 and Level 3 people to help senior managers build trust and accountability with their team members. The pilot was so successful that it rapidly got sucked down the layers of management to the frontlines. Soon the entire company was using the same process and the same single form. We subsequently went digital with what we called the "My PMP" program.

The speed of this dissemination around the world laid to rest the tired stereotypes such as "Asians are too polite" or "Latinos are too hierarchical" for the effective use of the PMP system. PMP helped us in our effort to become "one company, one culture, one team." Everywhere I went, whether it was Athens, Caracas or New Orleans, I noticed that our unified culture was helping us overcome internal divisions, allowing us, instead, to focus on customer care, the innovation pipeline and operational excellence.

We had similar PMP systems at my other companies. Our annual employee ranking systems at these companies did include the top 10 percent, the next 30 percent and the bottom 10 percent, with about half in the middle.[2] Also, our 30-percent number for the second category was higher than the conventional systems because we wanted more of our middle players to strive to get into this zone. We did not refer to our middle group as "average," or some other designation that would have devalued their contribution. *We wanted them to know they were valued contributors and to feel engaged in our mission.* The best ratings terminology I have seen as part of my experience is used at Bausch + Lomb, where I am currently chairman. (See Appendix D.)

Assessing and developing people is a basic leadership responsibility.

CHAMPION THE INNOVATORS

On October 17, 2012, I woke up to an e-mail from Merck's CEO, Ken Frazier. He had attended the prestigious Prix Galien ceremony the previous night and his company's Hepatitis C product, Victrelis, had won a 2012 innovation award. He was writing to congratulate me for championing Victrelis while I was at Schering-Plough. What made me really proud was that this virus was detected only recently (1989) and, thanks to advanced therapies that have taken cure rates to 75 percent, the CDC (Center for Disease Control) is now recommending one-time Hepatitis C testing for baby boomers. In America, 3.2 million are infected, and if undetected the disease can progress to liver damage or even death. It's moments like these that make it even more worthwhile to champion the innovators.

The best innovation comes from creating a dynamic culture by taking disciplined risks, assembling people with different skills and

---

[2] This 10 percent included both the bottom sub-categories comprising those on a performance-improvement program and those deemed to have unsatisfactory performance.

ideas around a common dream, and curbing individual egos in favor of the collective team. I worked hard to surround myself with senior leaders who modeled the qualities of the Power Trident—Passion, Courage and Tenacity—and who also had good decision-making instincts and financial smarts. I was especially fortunate in attracting strong heads of R&D. By encouraging scientific pursuits and following through with disciplined product-development processes, we were able to leave behind stronger innovation-products pipelines than the ones we had inherited.

At SGP, our late-stage R&D pipeline went from no potential blockbusters in 2003 to five in 2008. Our R&D head, Tom Koestler, who joined us at SGP after the Pfizer/PHA merger, has probably the most prolific product-approval record in the industry.[3]

In April 2011 I was invited by my Big Pharma CEO colleagues to be a panel guest at their trade group's annual meeting, which included their annual Discoverers Award ceremonies. This event occurred at the Liberty Science Center in New Jersey. The previous Discoverers Awards, dating back to their beginning in 1987, were proudly shared in a handout. I, in turn, was proud to note that my previous R&D teams at Sandoz, Wyeth, PNU, PHA and SGP had been involved with nine of the product innovations on the list, an unusual number given that the industry total was 43.[4] Due to the long innovation process in the pharmaceutical industry, some of these product innovations were not launched while I was at those companies, but I am proud to see that my R&D teams were involved in making a difference for millions of patients around the world.

I represented Sandoz with great pride in October 1988 in Washington, DC, when Jean Borel was chosen by his industry peers to receive that year's prestigious Discoverers Award. At Sandoz, Jean single-handedly championed the development of cyclosporine, an innovative product to prevent the rejection of transplanted organs. The project could easily have been killed since the marketing

---

[3] New drug approvals by the FDA.

[4] Includes both pre- and post-initial-marketing phases.

department's sales forecast was low. For good reason however, pharma R&D is almost always separate and independent from marketing. Through his relentless commitment, which some called "a bit of insanity," Borel championed cyclosporine, ultimately leading to organ transplantation becoming a huge industry. Hundreds of thousands of people around the world are alive, or don't have to suffer debilitating kidney dialysis today, because of the passion and persistence of Jean Borel.

In large corporations, one can be sure there will be no shortage of naysayers. If you want to encourage innovation, sponsor people who are smart, who are passionate champions and who know how to build team alignment and execution. You must also fight victimhood. Victims are so busy feeling sorry for themselves that they don't innovate.

The leader's duty is to develop a culture that stimulates innovation, and to be proud of those who stay the course and turn their innovation dreams into reality.

USE THE KNOCKOUT SYSTEM WHEN EVALUATING SENIOR EXECUTIVES

I have interviewed thousands of internal and external job candidates during my unusually active life of cultural transformations, mergers and acquisitions. Making judgments about people is both an art and a science. Trusting your gut is good, but simple checklists also help.

Given the successful people who have worked for me, including six direct reports who later became CEOs of large public companies, I believe my batting average has been respectable.[5] However, hiring mistakes inevitably occur. When they do, one needs to exhibit high Leadership EQ in admitting a mistake and moving on to plan B.

---

[5] In alphabetical order: Lamberto Andreotti (Bristol Myers Squibb), Bob Essner (Wyeth), Bill Hawkins (Medtronic), Steve MacMillan (Stryker), Bernard Poussot (Wyeth), Dan Vasella (Novartis).

When selecting a candidate, consider her track record, knowledge, skills and experience to get her through the door, and note her attitude and behavior to determine if she is the best candidate for the job.

There are behaviors that either confirm a winning candidate or signal potential red flags. Questions to ask yourself when interviewing and evaluating a prospective candidate's acumen, attitude and behavior can be boiled down to three:

1. Is he trustworthy?
2. Does she know her stuff and stay ahead of change?
3. Does he have energy and does he build team trust and team energy?

Question 1 is best answered by looking at the candidate's track record, references and EQ. From those who have worked *for* the candidate, ask, "Would you want to work for him again?" If the interview is in an office setting, notice how he treats the admins. If it's in a restaurant, notice how he treats the people who work there.

Question 2 is also best answered by looking at track record. Additional questions to ask her are, "What major cutting-edge changes are occurring in her field of expertise?" "What turns her on about these changes?" "What has she done best, and when has she failed most?" "What did she do after she failed?" "Has she made any accurate calls that others did not foresee?" "Is she afraid of surrounding herself with talent that may know more about her domain than she does?"

Beyond valuing senior executives for their leadership skills and domain knowledge, I especially value those who have insight on growth corridors of the future, and future threats that may derail strategic thrusts. At PNU, for example, our Team at the Top recognized that while PNU's oncology innovation strength was in classical cancer chemotherapeutics—like doxorubicin, epirubicin and irinotecan—the future lay in less toxic, more gene-targeted medicines, such as angiogenesis inhibitors. This strategic thinking led to the company's critical acquisition of Sugen in August 1999.

Question 3 is especially important. "Energy creators" contribute to team energy, while "energy absorbers" suck it out. Even smart people can be energy absorbers. They usually have self-agendas, as opposed to team or company agendas. These candidates should be avoided.

In trying to answer question 3, look at the candidate's problem-solving ability and authenticity. For problem-solving ability, when it's his turn to ask questions, notice if he asks "How can I be a better contributor?" questions, or if he asks "What's in it for me?" questions. Does he show genuine curiosity about the company and what would be expected of him in the short term and long term? Does he have the courage to ask at least one tough question, or is he overly diplomatic? On authenticity, when asked about his past colleagues or companies, does he tear down others to build himself up? When asked open-ended questions, does he provide examples of when he rooted for others on the team?

Promotion criteria are somewhat different from hiring criteria. Beyond assessing business acumen, I usually ask myself five questions when making a Level 2 or Level 3 selection, or a Level 1 decision in situations where I am on the board of directors or an investor in the firm.

1. Does he have a high Leadership EQ?
2. Has she developed passion in her work and among other individuals?
3. Does he work well as a matrix leader, and does he create purposeful team energy?
4. Does she contribute to coaching and developing others?
5. Does he actively seek coaching for himself?

These five criteria are by no means proprietary to me. Variants of them are used by most large companies. Organizations look at both business acumen and attitudinal traits when selecting senior leaders. The attitudinal traits are often looked at as a simple average or a weighted average. I believe one should use a knockout system. If someone scores low in any one of the criteria, knock that candidate out. Not everyone starts a career with all of the above strengths, but if a CEO or a Level 2 misses in any of the five attitudinal criteria, that company's *tone* at the top will suffer and the culture will head downward toward mediocrity. Level 1 and Level 2 selection and retention decisions need courage, candor and the willingness to act on any deal breaker.

It is surprising that when it comes to the most important executive selection decision—the CEO—many board selection committees don't fully benchmark internal candidates against what may be the best out there. Having been fully benchmarked for the jobs I took at Wyeth, PNU and SGP, I have both experienced and witnessed the critical importance of benchmarking. A high batting average with executive-selection decisions is critical for serial success.

For the C-suite jobs, use the knockout if there is a miss on any of the five attitudinal criteria.

WORK ON THE PRODUCTS

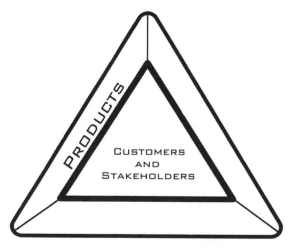

Ever wonder why some companies in product-driven industries do better than others? A dozen or so global products, or "product drivers," usually drive the top line in most global companies. Product-innovation CEOs or unit heads foster passion, courage and tenacity around these product drivers in their companies. The excitement they generate creates a positive contagion. These CEOs usually don't accept rearview market research.

I was at a product-development committee meeting at the Pennsylvania Wyeth Pharmaceuticals headquarters in 1995 when, during a presentation, I heard that "Europeans do not pay and will never pay more than $4,000/year for a biotech product like Enbrel." Weeks earlier, I had heard anecdotes that this product's astounding efficacy could have a dramatic impact on rheumatoid arthritis patients. We let the product development continue. Some years later, Enbrel hit the European markets in the double-digit price point range and, in many cases, above the U.S. price.[6] It is now well past $2 billion in annual European sales.

An obsession with products is an advantage if it is in the leader's playbook. Products make most companies relevant to their customers and consumers. A continuous run of new products and life-cycle management of existing products are important ways to keep customers interested. Existing products can be reinvented by improving them or through smart repositioning, repricing, rebranding or re-promoting.

One important engine for product maximization is to develop a culture that not only tolerates mavericks, but also provides them with a "surround sound" of positive people who support their work. While working at Dorsey Laboratories in Nebraska in the mid-1970s, I had to turn around the largest part of the company's portfolio, the Triaminic line of cough/cold products, in order to succeed in my new assignment as head of marketing. I knew that the turnaround needed someone other than the typical group product manager, so I recruited a frontline sales manager from the field, Terry Witt, for the job.

Terry had an intense personality, but he was creative. This was the first time Terry was in an office environment, and many people thought he was a maverick. I spent a lot of time covering and coaching him along the way. He was high maintenance, especially with the

---

[6] Over $10,000 per year.

R&D people, but the gamble paid off beautifully. Terry rebuilt trust with physicians and with the frontline managers. He revamped the formulation and positioning of the Triaminic line. We secured a turn-around within a year, which put Dorsey on a strong growth path.

An obsession with customers goes hand-in-hand with products. Our new culture at Schering Plough encouraged every employee to think of patients and other customers. By acting professionally and with integrity, every one of us could contribute to this common goal of earning trust.

In the pharmaceutical business, when a rep makes a sales call, the standard question from the doctor is, "What's new?" That's the same in almost any business. Those salespeople who can answer that question better than others improve their chance to be "invited in" the next time. Products—and news about products—help create relevancy with the customers.

An obsession with products will help build the team and the company.

WORK ON THE PROCESSES

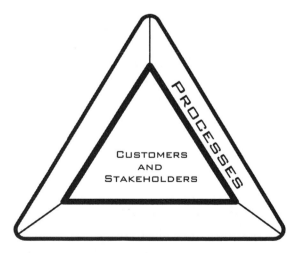

Processes are the third side of the Power Triangle. Horizontal work processes must be simple and robust so the output is predictable and realized at lower costs.

Creating process excellence requires paying constant attention to the *basics* that drive the organizations. Too often relatively sound organizations lose their way because they take their eyes off the basics.

Process excellence works best when there is *process discipline*. Many companies work on *skills* and *training* in order to ensure process discipline. They need to go even further. They need to insist on *attitudes* and *behaviors* that ensure a culture of process-driven work, whether it is cross-departmental, cross-divisional, cross–business unit or cross-hierarchy. This culture should require not only minimum organizational friction on cross-functional processes but also minimum deviations which remain well within prescribed tolerances.

Process mapping and simplification enables process excellence. Many companies struggle with getting it right. This struggle is compounded by the "process drift" syndrome that often occurs over time. This is when new subprocesses keep getting woven in and complicating the previously simpler processes. At all the companies I led, we focused on creating a strong internal culture to build and maintain process excellence. This meant having not only a few crosscutting "signature processes," such as our performance review system (PMP), but also "smaller" processes that would be more local to a country or a department. In a few cases we hired consultants, but mostly we relied on our own people to keep our basics robust and to upgrade the processes. In this way, we ensured that our people were committed to fighting "process drift" and to self-enforcing process discipline.

Under the joint leadership of Ian McInnes, head of Global Supply Chain, and Rick Bowles, head of Quality, we were able to launch significant process improvements[7] that lowered manufacturing deviations and rework and scrap costs (Figure 4.3 and Figure 4.4). Quality, customer service, cost performance and our relationships

---

[7] These included flowchart improvement, better validation of unit operations and improved training of frontline supervisors.

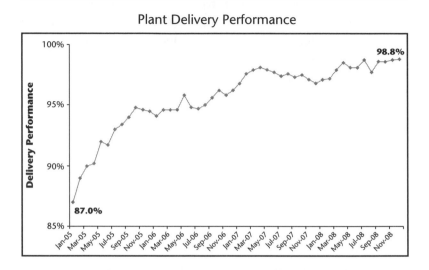

FIGURE 4.3   Increase in Delivery Performance

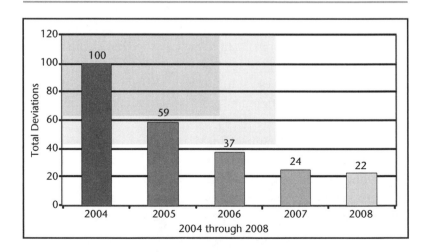

FIGURE 4.4   Reductions in Deviations Initiated

with regulators were all dramatically improved. Between 2003 and 2009, gross margins rose 600 basis points.

At SGP we also created enormous value for our innovation-products pipeline through our proprietary Customer-Centered Product Flow (CCPF) process. This signature process improved information fluidity and joint accountability among key R&D, commercial and manufacturing leaders. The process also created powerful mindsets by encouraging product and project champions and entrepreneurial and problem-solving behavior. In addition, once projects were promoted beyond a certain gateway, the process ensured a commitment of resources and relentless follow-through.

Finally, we worked hard on incentives to promote process excellence. For example, in order to signal to the country managers that they should contribute to and sign on to global processes and systems, as opposed to reinventing the wheel in each of their countries, their incentives included their contribution to the global network in addition to their local performance.

Sound processes and good process discipline contribute to building trust among people. They enable people to rely on each other to come through on process tasks and to free themselves up for more creative work.

DRIVE ENGINES OF INNOVATION

October 15, 2012, Alexandria Center, New York City: My co-panelist Dr. Roy Vagelos[8] and I had earlier been introduced as "two legendary CEOs" to this gathering of about 100 people consisting mainly of scientists and health policy experts. With great pride we discussed major medical advances—for example how, in the space of three decades since the identification of the virus, HIV has been turned from a death sentence into a manageable condition—thanks to innovative drugs. We also discussed how to create a culture where one can drive innovation while also attending to other priorities.

---

[8] During Dr. Vagelos's stewardship of Merck, it was repeatedly rated as "The Most Admired Company" by *Fortune* magazine.

Many large organizations succumb to the idea that operational excellence cannot coexist with innovation excellence. As a result, they prioritize operations and deprioritize innovation. However, both can thrive under the same roof if the CEO and the Team at the Top can develop a culture that allows this to happen. Senior executives should constantly strive to innovate and encourage new ideas, while maintaining the financial and process discipline to keep the basics strong, to follow through and to know when to cut one's losses.

Innovation includes resuscitating old ideas or even rejuvenating classic brands. There are many unpredictable pathways and iterative loops, from an original creative flash, to that "eureka" moment, to making end users delighted with an innovation.

I will never forget the day in 1987 when Dr. Jack Singer, who led psychiatry medicine at Sandoz (now Novartis), announced "Eureka!" and Clozaril, a new drug for schizophrenia, was reborn. Clozaril had been launched in Europe in 1971 and then pulled off the market in 1975 after a study from Finland reported that it caused a serious side effect, a sharp reduction of white blood cells, which could be fatal if not detected early, because it would lower the patient's immune defenses. The drug, however, also appeared extraordinarily effective in treating schizophrenia, and people in our U.S. operation did not want to give up.

A United States–led Skunk Works team started a dialogue with the FDA and received support to bring the drug back on the market provided the company could meet two tough conditions. Firstly, a strict "no blood, no drug" policy would ensure the drug was dispensed to patients only after they had cleared a weekly blood test. Secondly, Clozaril would have to clear the high hurdle of being effective on those patients who had failed on Haldol. Haldol was seen as the gold standard anti-schizophrenia drug. Once patients had failed with Haldol, the prognosis for these patients was generally grim, requiring very expensive state mental facilities where they would eventually live.

Our team worked to meet both these requirements. Carrie Cox, the talented business manager for Clozaril, who later joined me at WYE, PNU, PHA and SGP, developed the "no blood, no drug" system, and by 1987 we learned that Clozaril had beneficial effects for 30 percent of the Haldol failures!

I personally know patients who came back from the darkness of schizophrenia and reentered the community because of Clozaril—patients who can now live on their own or with their families, hold down jobs and defeat any suicidal tendencies. There is nothing more rewarding for anyone in health care than to see such small miracles happen.

Another unusual innovation led by a team at SGP gave new life to Dr. Scholl's, a 100-year-old brand that was primarily in the shoe-insert category. The team pioneered a FootMapping Technology that uses hundreds of pressure sensors to measure the areas of the foot that take the greatest pounding when walking. Then, the computer recommends a customized orthotics solution leading to the sale of a specific shoe insert from 14 alternatives (seven on each side of the machine). The self-standing, self-measuring machines were placed in high-volume retail outlets. The teamwork required to make this innovation happen extended to sites in New Jersey, Tennessee and China. All of the different groups and levels working on this project owned the innovation. Even the head of SGP's Consumer Health Care, Brent Saunders, personally followed up with Walmart to convince decision makers to place machines in their stores.

Now, more than ever before, innovation is a team sport that thrives on leadership and team energy. In the twenty-first century, knowledge in most disciplines has exploded. The solo innovators of the past now require functional experts to join the team and row with them. Innovators point to the island and then, in their role as innovation drivers, use their high EQ and team-building skills to get people to row the boat in the same direction and keep rowing even when the tide turns against them. As the starting point of the Executional Excellence Spiral, Earning Trust powers every effective innovation team, and it enables team members to work passionately together in order to finally arrive at the island.

A dynamic culture, led from the top, helps drive innovation.

WORK LIKE A SMALL COMPANY IN A BIG COMPANY

Bigness is both an opportunity and a challenge when it comes to innovation. It is an opportunity because it provides the financial scale to take on big projects and big risks. It is a challenge because large organizations tend to squash small, newly developed ideas before some of them move on to become major advances. It is also a challenge because smaller and nimbler competitors can disrupt the big company business model—as exemplified by Apple's apparent disruption of the music, computer and telephony industries.

Too many aspiring business executives in big companies go on to become defenders of the status quo. They believe, with some validity, that the surest way to be promoted is to avoid being blamed for a mistake. Bureaucracies and layers in large R&D organizations remain a challenge. In Big Pharma, for example, a company can have 10,000 R&D employees and multiple sites. Top-heavy organizational charts can dampen the enthusiasm of the inventors, many of whom are under 35 years old. That said, some large companies, such as Genentech and 3M, have done an admirable job of creating a "small company in a big company" culture.

Managing bigness needs active culture-change leadership from the top.

In addition to championing small projects and programs, the challenge of size can also be combated by encouraging the high-performance behaviors described in Chapter Five. These include matrix skills such as encouraging people to properly anchor with their colleagues and supervisors, to pursue initiatives and to be able to access the necessary resources by plugging into the power grid. Large organizations have to fight hard against the supertanker culture, whose weight becomes a drag on details, creativity and meeting deadlines.

Keep the organization's culture attuned and vibrant. Make sure you know if your innovators are someone else's disrupters, and if they too should be watching out for a potential disrupter. If they see early signs of an incipient threat, prepare your own competitive innovation as a response.

By behaving like a small company in a big company, you will encourage your team to be both strong and nimble.

Chapter Four Takeaway

Pick strong people, align them and motivate them. Superior products, processes and innovation will follow.

Chapter 5   Role Model Your Expectations

The second change-leadership takeaway in making the team stronger is to *role model your expectations*. This means role modeling winning behaviors and expecting leaders to lead and to build trust.

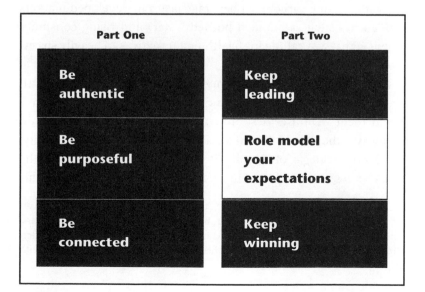

Part One	Part Two
Be authentic	**Keep leading**
Be purposeful	**Role model your expectations**
Be connected	**Keep winning**

DEPLOY THE LEADERSHIP QUARTET STRATEGIES

On a cool evening in Miami in March of 2006, I stood on the terrace of the InterContinental hotel with The Coca-Cola Company CEO, Neville Isdell, and other company executives. Neville had been called out of retirement to take charge as CEO to tackle a series of challenges that Coca-Cola was experiencing, including the departure of two CEOs. After hearing of my turnaround stories, Neville invited me to Miami to share my experiences with his global leadership team of about 200 top executives assembled there for a special turnaround meeting that would begin the following day.

I started my presentation explaining that every turnaround and transformation was different, yet my Playbook basics had worked for me at all the companies where I had worked. Before sharing my Playbook basics, I told the audience that in my estimation, the management team of Coca-Cola had the attitude, the humility, the open-mindedness and the passion that it would take to make this global icon great again.[1] I added that Coca-Cola's team was poised to exploit the opportunities in emerging markets, while also dealing with shifting carbonated beverage tastes in developed markets (via entries such as branded bottled water) and rising consumer activism that was calling for healthier alternatives to heavily sweetened beverages.

I then laid out the basics of my Playbook for them. "Start with productive attitudes and behaviors to build a productive culture," I told them. "Diffuse these into the organization via three main pathways: the *Power Trident* of Passion, Courage and Tenacity; the *Power Triangle* of People, Products and Processes; and the *Leadership Quartet* of four winning leadership approaches. Do this

---

[1] I certainly can't take any of the credit, but I'm glad to see that in recent years, The Coca-Cola Company has regained its sense of direction under the leadership of Neville and his successor, Muhtar Kent, whom I also spent time with at the meeting in Miami.

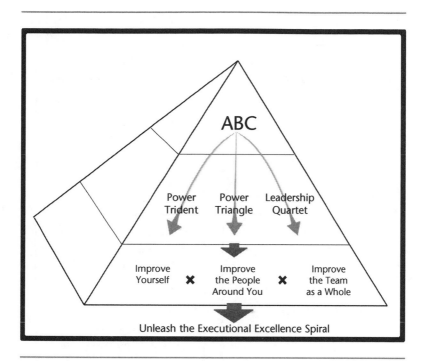

FIGURE 5.1   The ABC Diffusion Pyramid of Serial Success

right, and you can unleash a virtuous spiral of results that then generate even better results." During the ensuing Q&A, I became even more convinced that this company was upgrading its culture and would do well going forward.

The Leadership Quartet is the last of the three pathways, depicted in the ABC Diffusion Pyramid of Serial Success, that build a culture of enhanced productivity within an organization (Figure 5.1).

The Leadership Quartet, so called because all four elements are designed to work in harmony (like the four musicians in a quartet), was included in my Playbook to build trust and team effectiveness in the teams I led.

The Leadership Quartet

Lead with the Winning Team Formula	Embed the High-Performance Behaviors
Four pillars that enable the team to move with innovation, speed and flexibility.	Prominently displayed expectations of how successful colleagues will behave.
Use Situational Leadership	**Expect All Supervisors to use the Leadership Engine**
Expectations of supervisors to shift their leadership style depending on the situation.	Expectations of supervisors to coach and motivate each person they supervise.

The following four sections describe each of these four winning leadership elements.

Lead with the Winning Team Formula

"Oh! Johnny...Can You Stop Pakistan?" screamed the sports headline in the popular UK newspaper the *Daily Express* on the morning of Tuesday, August 17, 1954. Before becoming serious about his civil service career, my dad had been a good cricketer. He was now on assignment as manager of Pakistan's young cricket team, and I was along for the ride at a first-of-its-kind four-game series of test matches against the vaunted English team. England was up against a former colony, only seven years old, and was on its home turf in London's famous Oval stadium. England had managed to win one of the first three games, so Pakistan was going for a series tie against its heavily favored opponent.[2]

Source: Daily Express, August 17, 1954

Surprisingly, the expected blowout turned into a hard slog. The visitors did not have great fielding skills, but they were showing remarkable grit and team spirit. On this final Tuesday morning, England's hopes were resting on Johnny Wardle, their accomplished bowler who was also a good tail-end batsman. Emotions ran high. In the early postwar years in the UK, cricket garnered the same national euphoria as soccer does now, which is why this was a front-page picture story on August 17, 1954. For a while, a victory for the English side looked like a certainty, but, unfortunately for them, Johnny couldn't win the match for his side. Pakistan scored a shocking victory, a win that is still talked about by cricket fans to this day.

A few days later, I accompanied my father to a celebration held at a historic government house on the Pall Mall in London. Both teams were present (cricket does not respect sore losers), and I had a chance to talk to the famous English batsman, Denis Compton. I asked him how the unexpected had happened.

---

[2] The other two games had ended with no winners.

"We were too confident," he told me. "They were not only hungry, they were on fire."

I would never forget his words. When you witness a Winning Team Formula early in life, it becomes part of your playbook. I learned that being connected, confident, humble and energized *as a team* amplifies its collective power.

The Leadership Quartet begins with the first of four components: the Winning Team Formula.

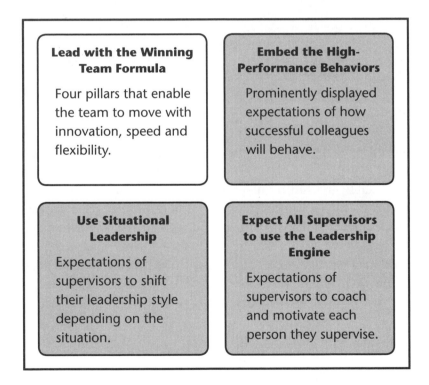

Lead with the Winning Team Formula

Four pillars that enable the team to move with innovation, speed and flexibility.

Embed the High-Performance Behaviors

Prominently displayed expectations of how successful colleagues will behave.

Use Situational Leadership

Expectations of supervisors to shift their leadership style depending on the situation.

Expect All Supervisors to use the Leadership Engine

Expectations of supervisors to coach and motivate each person they supervise.

A winning team in the world of business is built on the following four pillars:

1. *Setting clear goals* that unite and bind the team.
2. *Building faith* in the company's products, and sustaining faith in the top leadership and in yourself.

3. *Building knowledge, skills and training,* especially cutting-edge functional excellence that comes from preparation, curiosity, hard work and, whenever possible, practice.
4. *Embedding the will to win* and visualizing success together.

People who possess a winning attitude create positive energy around them. Their attitude is founded on a "can-do" spirit that makes them relentless in driving for success and finding joy in their work and in the success of their colleagues. In my CEO role, I sought out executive athletes or, more accurately, executive *pentathletes* for their passion for winning, functional excellence, business acumen, drive and ability to complement the skills of other team members. But attitude was always the prerequisite. People with a winning attitude find opportunities in challenges and inspire each other within the team.

At SGP we worked hard to promote this winning attitude—an attitude that would transform the company into an aligned, global, high-performance organization. We called it "one company, one culture, one team." Colleagues would strive to succeed beyond their own personal success. As in basketball, we sought to pass the ball to create the plays to score.

Winning is fun! And it leads to more wins.

Embed High-Performance Behaviors

Management by Objectives (MBO) is a powerful business concept that was introduced by Peter Drucker in 1954. Through the process of MBO, individuals identify the objectives that they plan to work toward, and they report their progress to a supervisor at predetermined times. With today's accelerating pace of change— even disruptive change—many of the more successful CEOs are deploying what I call *Leadership by Behavior,* which builds further on MBO.

At all of the companies I led, we emphasized high-performance behaviors, which, at SGP, we called Leader Behaviors. These behaviors set the expectations that would lead to a high-performance culture. At SGP, we posted them prominently at every company site and in all major languages. Our employees' Performance Management Planning (PMP) system had a section in its evaluation and coaching form that addressed the employees' high-performance behaviors. At least 20 percent of an employees' annual incentive depended on how well he or she lived up to them.

At SGP, we had our Team at the Top lead the way by modeling these behaviors with the expectation that the behaviors would cascade down to the frontlines. During a country visit to Seoul in South Korea, for instance, I saw that the local team had clearly adopted our behaviors. Not only did I see the customary wall posters on our behaviors, I could see the winning attitude in our people. The team energy and the good results I saw there made me realize that a strong culture drives outperformance in all areas of the business.

The high-performance behaviors clarified what people could expect of each other and how people should behave with each other.

SIX HIGH-PERFORMANCE BEHAVIORS

1. Sharing accountability and transparency
2. Encouraging cross-functional teamwork and collaboration
3. Listening and learning
4. Benchmarking and continuously improving
5. Coaching and developing
6. Exhibiting business integrity

The list of behaviors spread fast at Sandoz U.S., Wyeth Pharmaceuticals, PNU, PHA and SGP. The behaviors were not couched in exactly the same language, but the ideas were similar and presented in the same positive manner.

1. Share Accountability and Be Transparent: With shared accountability, all units and individuals who are engaged in a project or mission take responsibility jointly for accomplishing that project or mission, while fostering mutual respect and team spirit. When setbacks occur, the team and its leaders put the principles of high Leadership EQ to work and avoid finger-pointing or casting blame. People work hard to accomplish their tasks. In doing so, they do their best to avoid letting anything fall through the cracks. Work is completed in a timely manner with quality and creativity because high-performance behaviors solidify interpersonal contacts and build trust. Course corrections along the way become easier when people take joint ownership.

Since all my former companies emphasized "shared account-ability and transparency" as a key high-performance behavior, some may argue that "individual accountability" might have been affected. In fact, it was reinforced because individuals were expected to get their own jobs done as well as share accountability and be transparent whenever such behavior was needed to make the team more effective. Team behavior is increasingly needed to provide a competitive edge. Also, this does not mean creating a culture of micromanaging; delegation is essential for effective leadership. It does mean having people and processes in place to achieve stated goals.

When people know about productive behaviors, and know that these behaviors are practiced by their colleagues, team productivity goes up.

2. Encourage Cross-Functional Teamwork and Collaboration: In any complex and global business, cross-functional teamwork and collaboration are required to deliver high performance. No one individual has all of the requisite expertise or acumen. People need to be empowered to seek answers to issues and cut across boundaries to resolve cross-functional issues.

The power of teamwork is better harnessed by first choosing people with the right attitude—people who are comfortable with sharing information and ideas and asking colleagues for their opinions, without feeling inadequate or defensive.

In twenty-first-century organizations, certain matrix skills are needed to overcome the silo barriers of conventional cultures. By way of example, it was not long after arriving at Schering-Plough that I knew I had to break some glass. I reduced the number of corporate aircraft from four to two, and took many other actions that shook up the status quo. Probably the one decision that startled management the most was eliminating the executive dining room. The sight of the new CEO in the cafeteria, standing in line with his own tray, chatting with people, had a huge effect in confronting the horizontal and vertical silos.

Culture change was not only about eliminating executive perks, but also about bringing "positive perks" to the organization, such as replacing the company's "business" dress code with a "business appropriate" dress code. We told our people that we trusted their judgment. They came through. We rarely wasted time adjudicating in this area. We did remain traditional on some principles, though. We proudly remained laggards, for example, when it came to business dress requirements for our sales reps, even in areas like Southern California where doctors tended to be casually dressed. And, unlike almost all our peers, we did not take Friday afternoons off in the summer. The reason was clear: the building of cross-functional team solidarity would be compromised if people in the field generating the revenue worked all day on Fridays while those in the offices did not.

Collaboration soon became one of our critical core competencies. A major accomplishment at SGP was a "best practices transfer" across departments. The same Quality Management System we used to transform our manufacturing and quality assurance operations, first in the United States, then in other countries, became the inspiration for upgrading our clinical, laboratory and regulatory operations in our various global sites. Lateral thinking became an established expectation as we worked hard to smash the boundaries. We had to work on it—every day. If not actively countered, corporate cultures tend to drift toward turf behavior.

Most gratifying were the thank-yous I kept receiving from colleagues as I traveled to various sites around the globe. Shared accountability and transparency had not only increased their productivity, it had made their work lives more fun.

Tear down the boundaries to unleash the collective power of the team.

3. Listen and Learn: Part One of this Playbook focused on active listening and active learning as important tools for individuals to excel as leaders. These are high-performance behaviors that the entire organization expects from all of its members. They require an environment in which people actively solicit and openly share ideas, feel comfortable telling each other the truth as they see it, demonstrate high EQ in accepting negative feedback and foster the tools to actively listen and actively learn.

Role modeling by every member of the Team at the Top is very important in building a listening and learning culture. Supervisors' egos can prevent them from seeking the counsel of their subordinates. This is a mistake. Getting help from all directions not only demonstrates high EQ, but also signals to others that it is a good idea to ask for help.

Make listening and learning central to productive behaviors.

4. Benchmark and Continuously Improve: Benchmarking means comparing various elements of the operation against those of the best competitors with the goal of continuously improving. No matter what it is called, *unrelenting* continuous improvement is a mindset of companies that aspire to stay ahead. Competitive benchmarking and continuous improvement was part of my Playbook at Sandoz U.S., Wyeth Pharmaceuticals, PNU, PHA and SGP.

In my detailed conversations with many executives, I don't hear the term *benchmarking* as much as I would like. Among companies that grow big from their previous successes, it seems like benchmarking is used less and less. Successful cultures still need to strive to become better. Many of today's meandering giants could have been, in their past, more attentive to culturally enhancing practices such as benchmarking.

In Miami in October 2000, we were at our first Global Leadership Team (GLT) meeting after the PNU/Monsanto merger in March 2000. I explained the following philosophy to the 350 leaders assembled at this meeting:

> Make candid assessments, and keep making positive changes. Even after reaching a competitive benchmark, keep improving and, ultimately, create a

benchmark of your own for competitors to follow. It has to become a daily mindset. It's fine to ask, "Have I made my budget for the month?" but it is more important to ask, "How does my performance compare to the competition? Am I losing market share while making the budget?" Likewise, you might think you are hiring the best talent available, but what is the basis for such an assumption? What benchmarking was undertaken before the hire?

Benchmarking is also an expression of humility. Constantly measure your department or company against its smartest—not necessarily its largest—competitor, and against the highest-performing companies in other industries.

Use benchmarking in every element of the business, so that the team can continuously improve.

5. Coach and Develop Others: Just as actively listening and learning can help make the individual strong, coaching and developing others can help make the entire organization strong.

At SGP we signaled that nurturing talent and helping colleagues was every person's job. By publicizing this expectation and making it part of every employee's Performance Management Program (PMP), we greatly improved professional development.

Coaching and development is an active practice not only between supervisor and employee, but also between any and all sources inside the company. Some of my own best coaching came from the frontline managers during the hundreds of "CEO dialogues" I conducted at the different organizations where I worked. Frontline managers have their fingers on the pulse of the business and what competitors are doing. By listening to their candid feedback, I was able to learn and develop in my own job.

Encourage coaching and development of others as a building block of team power.

6. Start with Business Integrity: In Part One, I discussed business integrity as a competitive edge for the individual. The same applies to organizations. Business integrity binds the other five high-performance behaviors into a powerful single platform that cuts across geographies.

How do you ensure that employees are behaving with business integrity? It is impossible to be totally certain, but a good way to start is to hire people of good character and explain through role modeling and repeated communications how they are expected to behave.

In large organizations with tens of thousands of employees spread among dozens of countries, there will always be someone trying to take a shortcut, no matter how many times he or she is warned against it. No system can watch over all individuals all of the time. The best business integrity happens when people watch themselves. That's why making many detailed rules does not seem to work as well as a principles-based system supported by best-practices training. For one thing, rules can be confusing, and, for another, some people may be tempted to look for ways around them, or may be confused when facing a decision that does not seem to be covered by them. Expect people to follow their own moral compass, and expect the senior management team to lead by example. Learning can also be supplemented by conducting educational discussions using hypothetical case examples.

High-performance behaviors, clearly articulated, understood, role modeled and expected, helped me to unleash productivity at all the organizations I led.

Use Situational Leadership

During a beautiful Indian summer afternoon in 1973 in the Pocono Mountains of Pennsylvania, I was at an off-site meeting when Fred Meyer, the senior finance and strategy vice-president at Sandoz, told us, "Be a seagull; fly high and see the big picture, then dive deep to catch the fish."

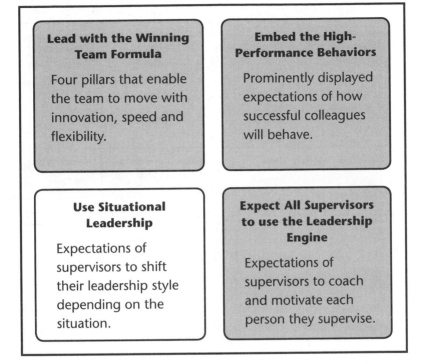

I liked the metaphor. Knowing when to leave matters alone or when to dive deep is a crucial situational leadership skill that I have tried to develop throughout my career.

The Situational Leadership Model (Figure 5.2) demonstrates a spectrum of leadership styles available to leaders. High-Leadership-EQ supervisors make appropriate decisions about what leadership style to use in various circumstances.

At one end of the spectrum is autocratic management, in which the leader of the team makes decisions alone. This paradigm is appropriate, for example, during a crisis situation that requires fast and decisive action or where there may be compliance or regulatory issues.

At the other end of the spectrum is laissez-faire management, in which decisions are made by individuals or the team without consulting others or a leader. This paradigm is appropriate in

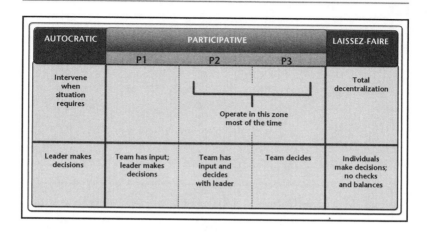

FIGURE 5.2   Situational Leadership Model
Source: SGP/Merck

circumstances such as highly structured routine activities. Most of the important decisions that relate to complex, nonroutine issues will fall into the P1, P2 and P3 zones, and will be made using a participative-management approach that requires shared-accountability behavior.

In some cases, the team discusses activities and then implements the activities that are decided upon, and the leader is subsequently informed (P3). In other cases, the team discusses and recommends a decision to the leader and waits for a final endorsement before implementing its plan (P1). In still other cases, the leader might participate as a member of the team, and together the team discusses and then implements the decision (P2).

Companies should operate in the P2 and P3 zones most of the time. Participative decision making helps to speed implementation and ensure that dialogue occurs, ideas are voiced and final decisions have maximum alignment.

Situational leadership also includes:

1. Owning processes jointly
2. Being a passionate driver

3. Having road maps
4. Role modeling
5. Turning adversity into opportunity
6. Following through with purpose

1. Own It—Jointly: Under the conventional process of turning strategy into execution, some people chart the company's direction, others communicate down the line and, finally, the frontline managers put the plan to work. In large companies this conventional "handoff" system can create a "my work is done, it's your problem" mentality. I thanked my Dorsey colleagues at an R&D gathering in 1980 because even after they had passed on the primary responsibility of a project task, they retained a sense of joint ownership. I pointed out to them that this cultural transition was already working in helping us to spawn very effective life-cycle management of products coming out of R&D because of our unusual team spirit between R&D and commercial. I gave them the example that after the unexpectedly successful launch of the antihistamine Tavist in 1978, we had followed through with an antihistamine plus decongestant combination called Tavist-D, which greatly leveraged the original Tavist franchise.

One thing that may have set me apart from many other executives was my heightened curiosity and relentless probing whenever someone's leave-me-alone attitude raised a red flag. The message I wanted to send was that there should be no protectiveness. Any strong manager should be able to withstand probing—in fact, he or she should welcome it.

I also worked hard at encouraging an atmosphere where the messenger did not get shot, where admitting a mistake was a badge of courage and where bad news would travel fast to those who needed to know.

Sometimes decisions can be so complex or controversial that the leader must gain alignment and avoid surprises with the people who could be affected. In that case, the leader encourages candor during the input and decision-making phase, which "anchors" the decision with those parties who may be affected later. I was very insistent on team unity at all the turnarounds I led. I told my team that there may be differing opinions, but, once a decision was made, we would insist on passionate and unified execution.

Even if there is 75-percent agreement, once a decision is made there must be 100-percent alignment on getting the job done!

2. Be a Passionate Driver: At Sandoz U.S., Wyeth Pharmaceuticals, PNU, PHA and SGP, we expected every supervisor to become a passionate driver by:

- *Knowing the way.* Know what and how to execute while understanding the macro environment and the strategies being implemented.
- *Showing the way.* When appropriate, show people that you can get into the nitty-gritty of the business by showing them the *how.* Show them you are not afraid to make the tough calls.
- *Going the way.* Be visible. Stay with people and motivate them until together the team reaches success.

Starting at the top with credibility and authenticity is the key to exhibiting these qualities. One of my Playbook priorities during my early years was to try to learn the business from the frontlines. I asked for operational experiences and assignments so I could get my hands dirty. I also worked hard on my knowledge of the business fundamentals and the macro environment, so that I could gain strategic insights and anticipate events as much as possible. By digging deeply, I gained credibility as a leader.

Leadership by behavior builds credibility.

3. Develop a Road Map for Success: At almost all operations that I led, I laid out a graphically visible road map in the form of a Gantt chart so as to create a sense of a shared journey.

At SGP, a six- to eight-year action agenda was our long-term road map for success. Every December, I would show the company's progress against the long-term road map at a global town hall meeting. I would also share a brief assessment of my progress against each of my four or five major objectives for the year, and introduce my four or five objectives for the next year. I insisted that all the CEOs' objectives be articulated on a single page. We then asked all supervisors to create, in writing, their own action plans. The supervisors would then present their respective plans to their teams. This goal alignment cascaded down to the frontlines. At frequent intervals, supervisors were expected to compare their progress versus objectives, so as to contribute to the organization's commitment to execution.

A team's productivity increases significantly once everyone buys into and converges around the road map laid out for the company, for the team and for the individual.

4. Role Model the Excitement: Modeling conviction and enthusiasm has to start with the CEO and the Team at the Top. In most companies, these are the seven to ten top leaders, including those in charge of the major operational units.

As members of the Team at the Top demonstrated that they were the attitude carriers, behavior carriers and culture carriers, and that they sang from the same sheet of music, we gained authenticity with the rest of the organization. We were effective in developing a new and more effective culture. It then became easier to ensure that new hires at other levels met common criteria to ensure that they would keep adding to the new culture. Figure 5.3 describes the four-team system to model the excitement.

Beyond the Team at the Top, we extended this same cohesive spirit to an Operations Leadership Team (OLT), which consisted of the organization's top 35 or so executives in charge of the operational accountability centers that would help us in our transformation effort.[3] They included the heads of the major businesses, such as Consumer Health Care and Animal Health; the heads of the major

---

[3] Called OMT at some of the companies I led.

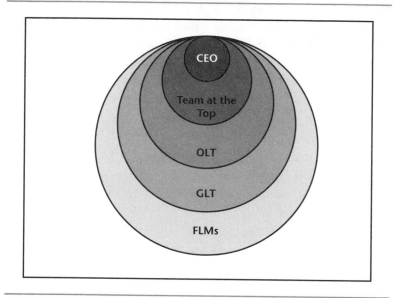

FIGURE 5.3 Accountability Teams

regions, such as Europe, Asia and Latin America; major product groups, such as Primary Care and Specialty Care; and the heads of global functions, like Manufacturing, Pharmaceutical Sciences and Toxicology, Clinical Research and Quality. The OLT met before the end of every quarter so that each accountability center could describe its progress versus its internal targets, and versus its competition. They also heard from me as the CEO on the latest developments and my ongoing expectations of them. Although there was a lot of content and discussion, we rarely let this quarterly meeting go beyond four hours.

We worked hard to ensure that all OLT members were fully committed to the action agenda. At SGP's first meeting with this group in December 2003, I promised them that the passion, courage and tenacity that we expected of ourselves and our people would lead to the envisioned turnaround and transformation. I then discussed accountability.

"If you miss your sales target," I told them, "instead of blaming the competitive situation, think, 'I should have known our competitive situation was difficult and should have worked even harder on honing the selling skills among my people.'"

The next accountability team was the Global Leadership Team (GLT), consisting primarily of country managers who, whenever necessary, could "plug into the power grid" of our global enterprise. I developed close relationships with many of these individuals. Our focus on building a cohesive GLT enabled the company to be strong both globally and locally.

The fourth accountability team, the frontline managers (FLMs), were ambassadors from the center, as opposed to many conventional large enterprises where they were so distant from the center that they seemed more like shop stewards.

In populating these accountability teams, the ability of individuals to embrace transformational culture change became a requirement for selection. Once everyone understood the new criteria, it became easier to:

- encourage the "culture carriers";
- move out the "culture rejecters";
- convince and convert the "fence sitters"; and
- confront the "passive-aggressives," and force them to make the choice of whether to stay on the train or get off.

During culture change, the passive-aggressives need the most work, since they may say they are on board, but they may actually do very little to support culture change, or may even quietly subvert it.

Culture change is the hardest thing to accomplish at long-established companies. But once the leadership teams model the excitement and make culture change really happen, the virtuous Executional Excellence Spiral kicks in powerfully.

5. Turn Adversity into Opportunity: Adversity is part of life and part of business. By dealing with life's curveballs, we become stronger and more resilient. We become more confident because we know we have been tested.

When I took on the additional responsibility of R&D at Wyeth in 1990, I knew we badly needed a big win from our internal R&D department. Wyeth had built a reputation in the three earlier decades as a great in-licensor of products from European companies. Now these companies had started their own U.S. operations and were no longer out-licensors. We needed to produce a great compound from our own kitchen.

Our labs had developed an aldose reductase inhibitor (ARI) called Alredase (tolrestat), a novel compound that appeared to block the disease cascade that led to long-term organ damage from diabetes. The early data indicated new hope that Alredase would protect diabetes patients from the years of damage to the eyes, kidneys and nerves. The global diabetes problem was so great that many countries approved Alredase based on the early data, and the drug reached the market in those countries.

In the United States our hopes remained high as we embarked on a clinical study involving large numbers of diabetes patients. Optimism was not limited to Wyeth. The University of Miami's Diabetes Research Institute was so enthusiastic about Wyeth's diabetes research that it asked me to cut the ribbon at the opening of its new facility in 1994.

Then came the heartbreak. When this study data was finally unblinded, it didn't show the benefit we were looking for. We will never know whether it was the underlying disease cascade hypothesis or the molecule itself, or even the study design that caused the surprise. In spite of protests from doctors and patients, our R&D head did the right thing in deciding to take Alredase off the market in countries where it had already been approved. We operationally wrote off hundreds of millions of R&D dollars.

The adversity that this event created made us hungrier in our efforts to develop other drugs. Eventually the "Class of 2000" at

Wyeth unveiled new drugs with a far greater impact on human health than even tolrestat would have had.

Sometimes turning adversity into opportunity is as simple as a newcomer turning a difficult situation into purposeful change that sends a powerful signal. When I first arrived at PNU, the company had some magnificent facilities, including Krusenberg Manor, a beautiful seventeenth-century mansion located in the rolling country north of Stockholm. A long tree-lined drive formed a graceful approach to the building. There were formal gardens and an apple orchard that led to a huge lake in the back, with another building and a boathouse. PNU was rightfully proud to have this showpiece for hosting events, and could boast of a renowned chef who attracted others to rent the facility for special events. The company also owned a hunting lodge in the far north of Sweden, where PNU executives enjoyed moose hunting; a hotel in downtown Kalamazoo, Michigan, with an "Upjohn Suite" reserved for the CEO; and Brook Lodge, a multibuilding country retreat outside Kalamazoo with yet another set of beautiful grounds and a lake. At the world headquarters in Windsor, near London, executives were served breakfast and lunch every day by a staff that had worked for the royals (who lived close by at Windsor Castle). Wow! As the new CEO of PNU, my lifestyle would be fabulous!

But that was not the message I wanted to send. If we were serious about saving PNU, all these facilities had to go. Their sale and the divestiture of others like them became some of my tough calls after I showed up at PNU. The adversity of a company in trouble allowed me an opportunity to change historical perceptions of management—fast. Getting rid of such perks enabled me to build trust, because people knew these luxuries didn't belong inside the new PNU when those on the frontlines were being asked to make sacrifices.

Turn adversity into an opportunity to send a strong message.

6. Follow Through with Purpose: Vincent van Gogh is credited with saying, "Great things are not done by impulse, but by a series of small things brought together." Following through with purpose means taking actions every day and every hour with your ultimate goal clearly in mind.

At SGP we worked hard to build this sense of purpose. We used our customary "early constituency" gatherings after the closing of a transaction to start building unity and team energy. For instance, at the frontline manager meetings in Europe and the United States (in November 2007 in Rome and January 2008 in Orlando), shortly after the Organon acquisition, I reminded these groups to reinforce *our common sense of purpose* among their teams. We followed through with purpose and made the Organon acquisition very successful.

By demonstrating positive energy, by thinking and acting and by positively communicating with one's team, each member of the team can mobilize resources and reach a higher level of success than might have been thought possible.

Follow-through is key to execution. Strategy is important too, but execution is 80 percent of success.

Situational leadership, in addition to the other three elements of the Leadership Quartet, adds strength to the team.

Expect All Supervisors to Use the Leadership Engine

Supervising others is a special responsibility. In fact, it should be treated as a special privilege. For any business, large or small, to have employees led by supervisors who are only ordinary, or worse, mediocre, has a sustained and severe impact on levels of pride, frustration, morale, initiative, passion and commitment. As I will discuss later in this chapter, you have to cut people loose who are endangering your organization or whose core attitudes and competencies no longer align with your firm's core business strategy.

This brings me to the final element of the Leadership Quartet: expecting *all* supervisors to use the Leadership Engine.

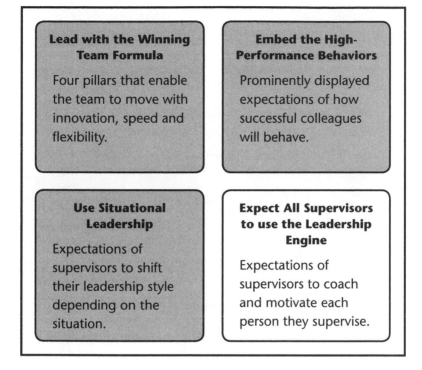

Lead with the Winning Team Formula	Embed the High-Performance Behaviors
Four pillars that enable the team to move with innovation, speed and flexibility.	Prominently displayed expectations of how successful colleagues will behave.
Use Situational Leadership	**Expect All Supervisors to use the Leadership Engine**
Expectations of supervisors to shift their leadership style depending on the situation.	Expectations of supervisors to coach and motivate each person they supervise.

What made all the companies I led different was that not only did we make people accountable to their supervisors, *we made their supervisors accountable to them.* We repeatedly told people that they should expect their supervisors to earn their trust as their leader, and to use the Leadership Engine (Figure 5.4).

Implementing the Leadership Engine within an organization helps to amplify the effectiveness of individual supervisors and the people they lead. It provides supervisors with a reliable template that serves to unleash the energy of each person they supervise. When given this kind of individualized leadership, people feel more valued. They feel that they can do more than they ever imagined. That helps to create a "do your best" commitment.

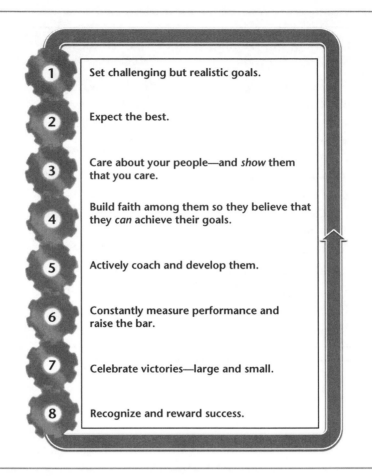

1. Set challenging but realistic goals.

2. Expect the best.

3. Care about your people—and *show* them that you care.

4. Build faith among them so they believe that they *can* achieve their goals.

5. Actively coach and develop them.

6. Constantly measure performance and raise the bar.

7. Celebrate victories—large and small.

8. Recognize and reward success.

FIGURE 5.4   The Leadership Engine
Source: SGP/Merck

My first application of this was during my early years in Lincoln, Nebraska, when I was suddenly leading many executives who had previously been my peers. The Leadership Engine worked very well in gaining their individual commitment and accountability, and the executives went on to apply the same cycle of motivation to their direct reports.

The Leadership Engine has eight distinct steps.[4]

This cycle of motivation was widely publicized at practically all the companies I led. As the Leadership Engine became embedded in successive levels of supervisors, and especially the frontline managers, more supervisors became effective leaders.

Set Challenging, Realistic Goals—Then Expect the Best: We generally found that with a strong and trusting culture, there was little difficulty in getting employees to be aspirational in their goal setting. Challenging but realistic goals were stretch goals that, assuming good alignment, training and execution, would still have more than a 50-percent probability of being achieved.

As mentioned earlier, at SGP I started with my objectives first. I shared my four or five major objectives for the coming year at a global town hall meeting early every December. These were subsequently aligned and cascaded through the company until everyone had their own objectives for the upcoming year. We expected all colleagues to have their own clear *line of sight* as a result of this cascading process. Some of the objectives didn't change much, year after year, but they still needed to be discussed and communicated.

Care about Your People, and Show Them That You Care: People are more likely to give their best when they believe their leader cares about them and has confidence in their abilities.

Build Faith and Actively Coach and Develop Your People: An important expectation of each supervisor is to build faith in the mission and in his or her people's own abilities. Employees will become more self-confident when they are actively coached and developed by their supervisors. Supervisors should encourage employees to practice, to learn and to keep getting better at what

---

[4] This descriptor was used at SGP. There were other descriptors at other companies, but the cycle of individual supervisory leadership worked in the same way.

they are doing. Coaching and mentoring can make people go from good to great. A supervisor's ability to excel as a leader increases if she builds trust and creates an environment in which coaching and mentoring are welcomed, and in which the employee also feels safe in giving feedback to his supervisor.

Once trust builds between the employee and his supervisor, the employee is motivated to expect the best from himself and to *give* his best. People think beyond the money when they trust their supervisor, find meaning in their work and feel that they are learning and growing. A trusting and learning culture is a loyalty maximizer.

Constantly Measure Performance and Raise the Bar: Measuring output is a powerful reinforcer of positive, purpose-driven work. Employees should know about their progress and be encouraged to feel that they have the power to raise their sights and aspirations.

After leading a company through a turnaround, I would turn the focus of our people to the transformation journey that still lay ahead. I told them to think like champions. I used the analogy of a coach who would tell the team at the after-game victory celebration to report to practice at 8 a.m. the next morning. Not only did this avoid excessive celebration and partying, it also provided a marker to all team members to stay focused on winning again and again—on being champions.

Celebrate Victories, Reward Success: By recognizing and celebrating victories, large and small, and giving credit where it is due, people feel fulfilled, valued and encouraged to strive harder on the next part of their mission. It is important to give recognition soon after the achievement has occurred. Praise should be expressed in the context of recognizing the attitude, behavior and hard work that produced results. It should not be false or inflated. If done in the presence of an employee's colleagues or peers, recognition will further motivate the individual. On the reverse side of the coin, criticism should be honest, yet empathetic, and almost always be conveyed in private.

Fair recognition and financial reward is "good hygiene" that contributes to motivated employees and organizational health. It completes the motivation cycle, and helps the next cycle to be even more powerful. I don't remember ever losing an A-player because he or she felt shorted on compensation.

By articulating clear expectations of the team, and by being a good role model for these expectations, one makes a good start in unleashing the power of we.

EARN TRUST BY MEASURING THE TRUST INDEX

An important role modeling step is to share with the organization how they feel and what can be made better.

After arriving at a new company, and then again two or three years later, I would look at the trust index—which is not only an indicator of the company's organizational health, but also an actionable diagnostic tool to make improvements. Auditors work hard at measuring the financial health of an organization, but most of those numbers are, in fact, lagging indicators. Organizational health is a leading indicator. Financial health is customarily audited, but senior management teams usually get a pass on organizational health audits. Not only should the factors in the trust index be measured, there should also be a pre-survey declaration that the results will be published—good, bad or ugly. This helps earn trust.

Trust is a subset of organizational health, and we would pose the following type of questions to ascertain levels of organizational well-being:

- Do I trust company management?
- Do I feel that I can win?
- Do I trust my supervisor?
- Do I feel that the company can win?
- Do I understand the strategy?
- Would I recommend my company if a friend was looking to join?
- Do I feel valued?
- Does this company value its customers?

- Is it safe to speak up here?
- Does this company value innovation and productivity?

The firm that we used at PNU and SGP, ISR, had a normative database against which we could compare ourselves. Figure 5.5 depicts the key "before" and "after" details in organizational health metrics at PNU and SGP.

ISR's lead expert, Jack Stanek, was surprised at the speed and the size of the organizational health improvements at both PNU and SGP. These dramatic improvements signaled a major upgrade in trust within the organizations and subsequently with customers,

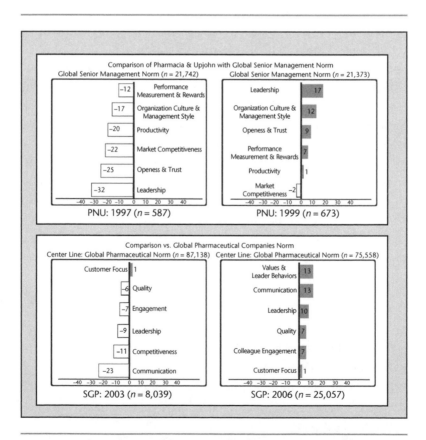

FIGURE 5.5 **"Before" and "After" Organizational Health**

lawmakers and investors. At both companies, the transformed culture drove strong execution, strong operating results and significant R&D pipeline upgrades.

A high Trust Index is important for high performance.

EARN TRUST WITH THE FRONTLINES

As mentioned earlier, a crucial role modeling ingredient in my Playbook involves a partnership with the frontline managers. Figure 5.6 is a graphical representation of "inverting the pyramid."

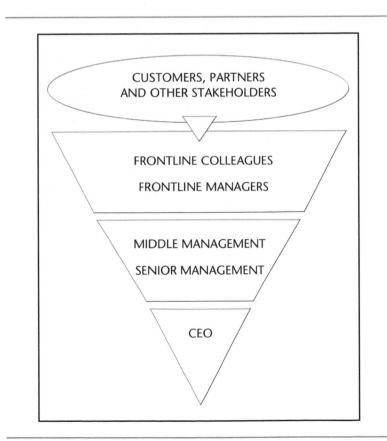

FIGURE 5.6   Inverting the Pyramid
Source: Bausch + Lomb

Why frontline managers? Because these first-level supervisors directly influence the motivation and morale of the people who do the work.

I focused on earning the trust of the frontline managers by showing *authenticity* on the part of senior management. I always made it a priority to educate the frontline managers about company strategy. This meant letting them in on what I had been talking about with my senior management team and even the board of directors, often using the same slides. Linking them into strategy this way prevents the frontline managers from becoming detached from the center, which occurs in many organizations.[5]

Beyond discussing strategy, we worked on other ways to *win the hearts* of the frontline managers. We not only wanted them to take ownership of the company's strategy, we wanted them to lead their frontline teams with passion, courage and tenacity.

Taking an interest in the frontline managers requires senior managers to allocate a portion of their time to this group, but the rewards are huge. We repeatedly reinforced the clear expectation that all members of senior and middle management were responsible for supporting their frontline managers, because they were the ones who, in turn, led the frontline workers. At SGP, even with 50,000 global employees, I was personally committed to reaching out to the 8,000 or so frontline managers via frequent CEO dialogues, letters, voicemails and video messages. To show our commitment, the first management-development program we established was the Frontline Manager Program, complete with practical tools such as speaker teacher kits to help the managers communicate with their people.

One thing I liked about the CEO dialogues with groups of frontline managers was that sometimes what seemed like a trivial issue or problem turned out to be surprisingly important. Take, for instance, an SGP CEO dialogue that I had in July 2006 with our frontline sales managers at our Russian operation. I heard a

---

[5] Part of this discussion was originally published in "Leading Change from the Top Line," *Harvard Business Review*, August 2006.

complaint about how long it took to get corporate approval to assign a company car to a new sales rep. I troubleshot the problem with my staff, but I also learned a lot more. Russia was in the middle of a war for talent because companies were discovering that Russia was in the early phase of a prolonged boom. We made Russia a priority, and ended up substantially improving our position in the Russian market—all because I had heard from the frontlines the need to be competitive in getting cars for sales reps.

Soon after taking charge at PNU in 1997, I visited our R&D facility in Uppsala, Sweden. I was shown a new delivery mechanism for our human growth hormone, Genotropin. Because the recipients of the hormone are children, making the delivery system as easy and as painless as possible was important. The prototype was a pen-like device with a spring-loaded needle that allowed for a quick injection. However, there was some concern because the device was intended to be injected into the belly, which children might find scary.

I was handed the saline-filled prototype so that I could admire its design. I startled my frontline manager colleagues by injecting myself. In part, I was gathering data. I immediately understood, for instance, that the injection could be administered so quickly that it would be over before most children had even focused on it. But I was also sending a message to the frontline. In seeing the CEO engage in such a visceral way, they understood that I really felt their job was important.[6]

Turning the organization's pyramid on its head helped accelerate the PNU turnaround in 1998. If people at the frontlines feel close to the CEO and senior management, purposeful energy gets generated where it matters the most. And whenever stressful conditions developed, as they always do, our cadre of frontline managers kept our workers calm and focused on their mission.

The frontline was also an important factor in the surprisingly successful integration and operational performance following

---

[6] The Russian car and Genotropin stories originally appeared in the article "The Frontline Advantage," *Harvard Business Review*, May 2011.

PNU's merger with Monsanto in 2000. A few days after the new company, Pharmacia, was born, we got the Monsanto and PNU frontline sales managers together—in the *same* meetings—in the United States and in Europe. Instead of spending a lot of time on administrative issues, my Team at the Top colleagues and I were out there with the frontline managers where it mattered. Building trust helped motivate them and, in turn, the reps they managed. Unlike many mega-mergers, we did *not* lose control of revenue during our merger process. In fact, we enjoyed healthy revenue growth and strong earnings-per-share (EPS) growth (19 percent compounded EPS growth between 1999 and 2002) during the last full year before the April 2003 merger with Pfizer.

In addition to the frontline managers, it is important to communicate regularly with all employees, and especially with the country managers in a large global enterprise. During my country visits, I made it a practice to travel without an "entourage," not only to avoid looking "imperialist," but, more importantly, to enable direct and informal exchanges with my country colleagues.

As I traveled to company sites all over the world, I almost always met the local country manager one-on-one for a substantial amount of time, and attended dozens of gatherings of company employees. As CEO of PNU, I surprised employees by sending them informal e-mails. This was in 1997, and it was a novelty for the CEO to send e-mail to company employees. I sent many under the heading "Talking about our business," which was one way to get all 30,000 PNU employees to feel closer to their CEO. It also conveyed the idea that, together, we were going to make this previously failing merger work.

At our Global Leadership Team (GLT) meeting in Copenhagen, in March 1998, I reminded the audience about energizing our frontline managers. I also told the 350 leaders that while our numbers didn't reflect it yet, I could see it in their attitudes that we were going to win. Seven months after that Copenhagen meeting, the October 30, 1998, *Wall Street Journal* carried the headline "Turnaround Becomes a Reality at Pharmacia & Upjohn."

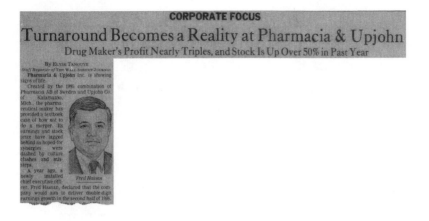

CORPORATE FOCUS

Turnaround Becomes a Reality at Pharmacia & Upjohn

Drug Maker's Profit Nearly Triples, and Stock Is Up Over 50% in Past Year

By ELYSE TANOUYE
Staff Reporter of THE WALL STREET JOURNAL

Pharmacia & Upjohn Inc. is showing signs of life.

Created by the 1995 combination of Pharmacia AB of Sweden and Upjohn Co. of Kalamazoo, Mich., the pharmaceutical maker has provided a textbook case of how *not* to do a merger. Its earnings and stock price have lagged behind as hoped-for synergies were dashed by culture clashes and missteps.

A year ago, a newly installed chief executive officer, Fred Hassan, declared that the company would aim to deliver double-digit earnings growth in the second half of 1998.

Fred Hassan

By inverting the pyramid you speed up the turnaround.

EARN TRUST WITH CUSTOMERS

Role modeling is especially important in customer care. Earning trust with customers begins by doing the right thing and doing it well. The customer experience at *all* touch points should be so satisfying and rewarding that customers will invite more contact. That kind of trust builds customer loyalty. Customer loyalty creates repeat business and the ability to build *market share at a discount.* As I write, Bausch + Lomb (B+L), where I am presently chairman, is working hard to become a trusted partner for eye health professionals, even though B + L is not the largest in its field. B + L pharmaceutical, contact lens and surgical representatives all support each other so that when they each call on the same customer, that customer gets an enhanced experience and begins to see B + L as a company that he or she can rely on.[7]

At the companies and business units I've led, we focused on excellence in five touch points, all coordinated to build trust through the customer experience.

---

[7] This example was featured in a complimentary article by Jonathan D. Rockoff, "Bausch Shifts Contact-Lens Focus," *Wall Street Journal*, April 25, 2012.

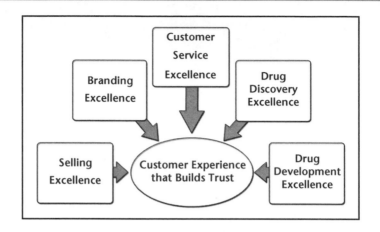

FIGURE 5.7 Transforming the Customer Experience—The Five Touch Points

We wanted our company, our sales reps *and* our individual products to stand out as trusted brands. Constantly changing messages or coming up short on delivery creates confusion and results in a trust deficit. We always wanted to give our customers a bigger reason to see us as their partner—beyond just buying or recommending our products. The vision statement in our core document focused on our organization being a *champion* for their cause. For example, at Schering-Plough we would demonstrate our commitment to earning the trust of doctors and patients by being a champion for better quality of care and better reimbursement.

A strong and authentic culture enables trust to be earned with the customers.

EARN TRUST WITH THE LAWMAKERS

As busy executives, many of us are tempted to gravitate to the comfort zone of our own operations and avoid working on the broader ecosystem, which includes the lawmakers, regulators and organized interest groups. Role modeling effective advocacy can be a differentiating skill among serially successful executives. Lawmakers are especially important.

Advocacy relies on trust building. Access must be sought via one's own stature and ability—as opposed to skirting the rules. If a level of trust can be established, one can get political leaders and their staff to listen better, even if they have different beliefs on core issues. In representing the companies or the industries in which I worked, I met many legislators and world leaders whose views on policy issues or on particular actions we were taking differed from my own. Earning trust and communicating our point of view was still important. For example, we were able to have a balanced conversation with the Italian government about Monsanto's genetically modified organisms (GMOs) in foods during a time when all of Europe was in a frenzy over the issue. I had a personal one-on-one with Silvio Berlusconi during an interregnum as prime minister, and felt assured that he knew and understood both sides of the issue.

Similarly, I built a high level of trust with Senator Max Baucus (D-Montana) who chairs the U.S. Senate Finance Committee. His keen intellect and curiosity built a relationship with me that extends well beyond the political issues of the day and has lasted over the years. In 2002–3, when I was chairman of Pharmaceutical Research and Manufacturers of America (PhRMA), he listened to our industry's advocacy for extending Medicare drug coverage to millions of seniors who were uninsured at that time. He defied his party's leadership and voted for what he believed was the right thing. His vote was vindicated when, a few years later, that program turned out to be more cost-efficient than expected, very effective in extending coverage to 90 percent of the seniors (up from 60 percent) and surprisingly effective in providing that care with good quality.

On my wall in my office in New York hangs a copy of the stamped official Senate action taken October 22, 2004, to allow for repatriation of billions of dollars of stranded American capital held in overseas banks. Senator Bill Frist (R-Tennessee), who was then the Senate Majority Leader, shepherded this move. He sent me the document with a personal note scribbled on it, recognizing my advocacy. Many important investments in the American economy resulted from this legislation. The $9.4 billion that Schering-Plough repatriated helped to keep the organization going during its difficult time, and later helped in its "Build the Base" phase.

Global business leaders stay tuned in to effective advocacy. They and their staff curb their egos and comfortably meet with authorities and legislators' staff at all levels.

EARN TRUST BY FOCUSING ON LONG-TERM VALUE CREATION

Role modeling for the long term builds trust.

Long-term investors have the time-arbitrage advantage over short-term investors. Yet short-term pressures are strong, and, today, companies' stock holdings can turn over as much as 100 percent per year or more. A strong quarter-end portfolio performance report or a year-end bonus for the fund manager sometimes becomes more important to him than encouraging his portfolio company CEO to build the business for the long term. Managers, like long-term investors, should go against this grain. Building strength for the long term stares you in the face at pharmaceutical companies in particular. About 70 percent of the business needs to be reinvented with new products sales from R&D every 10 years because of patent expiries. Valuing a pharmaceutical company based on quarterly earnings per share does not adequately reflect the true health of a business that runs on five- to fifteen-year R&D cycles.

At SGP, we became the only organization in our peer group to refuse to issue quarterly, or even annual, numerical earnings per share (EPS) guidance. We explained to our long-term investors that we wanted to create value for the long term. We also didn't think it would be authentic leadership to tell our own people that we were on a six- to eight-year transformational journey while, at the same time, speaking short-term talk to the outside world.

It turned out that this strategy was worth it. We had 17 straight quarters of double-digit sales growth. Even with some bumps on the road, our EPS went from just a penny per share in 2004 to

$1.75 in 2008. Our late-stage R&D pipeline went from no poten-
tial blockbuster in 2003 to five in 2009.[8] Not only did we succeed
in winning the trust of SGP's people, but we also won trust from
almost all of the long-term holders of SGP stock. Despite our lack
of numerical guidance, SGP's forward price earnings (PE) ratios,
based on analysts' earnings estimates, trended on the stronger side
compared to the Big Pharma norms. I heard from more than one of
our large investors that they wished more companies would hold
fast on avoiding numerical short-term EPS guidance.

Earn trust by communicating effectively on long-term value creation.

EARN TRUST IN MERGERS AND ACQUISITIONS

Role modeling in mergers and acquisitions (M&As) is important
as it is usually a period of accelerated change including uncertainty
and the breaking and forming of new relationships.

While mergers and acquisitions (M&As) often make strategic
sense because they allow companies to concentrate resources, gain
mass, increase efficiencies and spread the risk, about half of all big
M&As disappoint. The disappointments are usually blamed on
poor strategic fit, poor deal terms, poor deal timing or poor integration. An important reason that M&As fail to live up to expectations
is the managerial attitude behind the pre- and post-transaction
integration.

In mega-mergers, the larger company's executives usually come out
on top, and then often fail to remember the qualities and the talent in
the smaller company that made it attractive in the first place. It's like a
suitor telling his potential spouse, "I want to marry you for the qualities you have," and then after the wedding day, saying, "Now, be like
me" instead of, "Let's be something better, together."

Too soon after a transaction closes, CEOs feel the pressure to
declare "integration victory" after appointing new executives,

---

[8] All are operating (non-GAAP) numbers, including acquisitions/divestitures,
and are adjusted for special items.

combining the IT and accounting systems and eliminating redundant jobs. The cost-cutting part is usually the easiest part, and is almost always achieved in full or exceeded. The hard part is getting real buy-in on a shared dream, and holding the newly appointed leaders of the merged entity accountable for improving revenue and profit growth.

Another difficult piece is boosting the innovation trends of the *combined* legacy companies that were already in place before the transaction was announced. There is often a high attrition rate in the value of the merger if the revenue growth or the innovation doesn't keep up. Unfortunately, accountability for these kinds of post-transaction metrics often gets lost in the merger confusion, and short attention spans are inherent in the short-term investment cycles of many institutional investors. No wonder one in two mergers disappoints.

Building trust did work when we brought outside operations into our organization's fold. When Wyeth acquired majority control of Genetics Institute in 1992, one reason the deal closed at a reasonable premium (for both sides) was because of the relationship I had developed with the CEO, Gabe Schmergel. After the transaction we succeeded in keeping almost all of the Genetics Institute management team intact, and, as a result, the deal became a gateway to long-term growth for Wyeth biotechnology, organically and through subsequent acquisitions.

Similarly, PNU's Sugen acquisition in 1999 relied heavily on Göran Ando and me (then head of PNU's R&D) reaching out and engaging the Sugen management team. Sugen was a fiercely independent and innovative cancer company located in South San Francisco. We succeeded in retaining almost all of its key talent. We also kept our faith through their first three project failures, until Sutent (for kidney cancer) emerged as a significant winner.

Good integration begins with understanding the business and the values of the company that one is merging with or acquiring. At PNU, we sweated the details on Monsanto's business model, which included Monsanto's mission to improve agricultural productivity through biotechnology (through the use of genetically modified organisms). I developed a belief in Monsanto's mission. Thirty years earlier in Lahore, I had seen firsthand how improved seeds and fertilizers could make third-world farmers wealthier by bringing about a green revolution. In negotiating for Monsanto, I liked the Searle Pharmaceuticals business (including its R&D pipeline and its extensive product range, in addition to its already large antiarthritis drug, Celebrex). However, my empathy for agricultural biotechnology clearly helped. I was not intimidated by the anti-GMO fervor raging at that time in Europe (which included threats of physical harm to Monsanto executives).

Our Monsanto deal closed while other potential Big Pharma interlopers kept worrying about Monsanto's agricultural business. Even before closing, I reached out to the heads of Searle and Monsanto Ag and invited them to join the future combined company's integration team to ensure a successful integration. The Monsanto management team helped us to later launch a successful IPO of Monsanto as an agricultural company, and in 2010 Monsanto's CEO, Hugh Grant, whom I had always rated highly, was recognized as CEO of the Year by the Chief Executive Group.

When SGP announced the acquisition of Organon in March 2007, I distributed the dos and don'ts of integration planning to our operations management team (the top 35 executives at SGP). I told them that it would take many months to obtain regulatory clearances before we could close this huge deal. In the meantime, we would strive to earn trust with the Organon management in order to ensure a successful integration after we closed. I also told them that I expected this team to walk the talk when it came to respecting others, showing humility and learning about the new company before making any decisions and directives from on high. We also had our head of HR, Ron Cheeley, work with Organon executives to quickly develop a hate-to-lose (HTL) list, so we could approach these executives even before the acquisition was completed.

By walking the talk and by demonstrating high M&A EQ, we were largely able to prevent the "conqueror syndrome" that hurts the value of many M&A deals. In fact, the Organon acquisition surprised many by turning accretive in terms of earnings per share

(EPS) in the first full quarter after closing—an extraordinary outcome.[9] The Organon innovation pipeline also pleased us. Right through the acquisition and beyond, the flow of new-product approvals in countries around the world kept coming.

High M&A EQ is important in capturing the fullest value of a transaction.

EARN TRUST BY MAKING THE TOUGH CALLS

"You are a good person. We gave it a good try. Unfortunately, there is not a good fit between you and the job, so I have to let you go."

As leaders, we must make tough calls. It is an important role modeling action. These tough calls hurt even more when they involve people you really like. When I ran Sandoz Pakistan, I had to move out the head of the commercial operations. I had known him since high school! He was a good person but not the best for the job. I have had to make many such moves. It's no fun, but it must be done. Too often in organizations these types of tough calls get put off. For those being let go, early candor almost always turns out better than false compassion. I consider myself better than most at confronting reality early. In hindsight, I often think I should have brought in the right people for the right jobs even earlier.

Trust is made stronger by making the tough calls—even when they come as a surprise to the people involved. In July 1980, when I took over Sandoz Pakistan, one profitable (but small) business stood out. This was a business that grew and exported morels (specialty mushrooms) to Europe. Originally, Sandoz had installed farms in the Himalayas to grow the herb *Podophyllum emodi*, an active ingredient in a cancer treatment that had emerged from Sandoz's R&D division. However, that product had been out-licensed to Bristol-Myers, and the farms were now producing only these exotic mushrooms. I made the early tough call to exit this business because it was a distraction from the core pharmaceuticals

---

[9] As explained in the Author's Note, all sales and profit figures in this book are operating (i.e., non-GAAP) comparisons.

business that desperately needed help. I called in the senior executive of the business to give him the bad news.

"Why are you letting me go when I have worked so hard and helped build a successful business?" he asked me. I told him honestly that mushrooms were not core. He ended up going out on his own and doing quite well with a stand-alone morel business. The decision built trust among those who saw that I was focusing on Sandoz Pakistan's most important priorities.

One of the toughest calls a leader has to make is choosing which projects or programs to prioritize or to deprioritize. At most companies, many projects in the portfolio are not bad enough to kill or exit, but not good enough to get overly excited about, either. Often one hears, "If we could only spend more money, maybe we could get a breakout." Leaders have to set timetables or decision points and then follow through. While they should be passionate in driving projects, they shouldn't fall in love.

In fact, our R&D leadership often reminded us that one has to have "ice in one's veins" when evaluating projects. It advocated "killer" experiments, "to kill early, kill fast and kill often." For me, that meant killing early, but then really working hard on finishing those projects where a final late-stage decision point had resulted in a decision to make the prioritized investments and to expedite that project to the market. That strategy is how Merck was able to bring Januvia, the first DPP-IV inhibitor for diabetes, from its "first in man" study in 2002 to market launch in 2006, in less than half the time the typical project takes. Januvia is now a blockbuster.

Finally, tough calls need to be made to build an A-team. The first category of tough calls is in dealing with the *rock star*, an individual who does little to add to the culture and who may in fact be hurting team spirit. Make it a priority to give candid feedback *early*, and if he or she still remains a threat to the culture, then let the rock star go. Every time I did this, it built not only trust but also team energy.

The second category of tough calls is in looking at the *collective* strengths of the team. Look for the individual strengths of team members, and see how these individuals lead from their strengths while complementing the strengths of their teammates. If any individual is a mismatch or does not keep up, then, for the sake of the team, replace him or her with a better player.

Tough calls require courage. They help earn trust.

Chapter Five Takeaway

Through role modeling, expect winning behaviors, and expect leaders to lead and to build trust.

Chapter 6   Keep Winning

The final takeaway in making the team stronger is to keep winning. This includes fostering team trust and alignment, executing for results and driving the virtuous spiral upward.

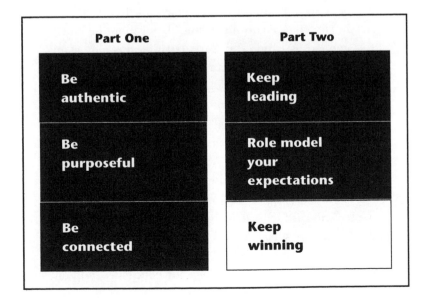

Part One	Part Two
Be authentic	**Keep leading**
Be purposeful	**Role model your expectations**
Be connected	**Keep winning**

USE THE POWER TOOL

Fostering trust and team alignment is a power tool that will enable you to gain the ABC Advantage. At companies large and small, a lack of mutual trust and alignment is a big productivity derailer. When there is a trust deficit, information is either hoarded or it stagnates; it doesn't travel up, down or sideways. People lower down in the ranks are afraid that their careers will suffer if they speak up, take a risk or act boldly. At senior levels, people often scheme about how to maneuver to the next personal opportunity. In many culturally challenged companies, people in power collect weaker people near them because "yes-people" make them feel comfortable.

Improving trust and alignment was my message to the newly constituted Schering-Plough Global Leadership Team (GLT) of about 350 leaders at its first meeting in Parsippany, New Jersey, in December 2003. "Trust and alignment will allow all of us to work together at a higher level. With a team effort we can achieve a quantum jump in productivity." I also told them that

> Having become trustworthy does not mean we can now get back to old attitudes and behaviors. Relationships need maintenance and nurturing; they cannot be taken for granted. We need to earn trust again and again among each other, our customers and our owners. Being accountable is part of how one builds trust. People around us will make their judgment about us based on our attitudes and behaviors. *And if our attitudes and behaviors live up to the values we espouse, then we earn trust that is long lasting and authentic.* We will always be more successful if we have our subordinates, our peers and our supervisors rooting for us. We cannot force alignment—we have to earn trust first. Relationships do matter. We don't need to socialize with everyone. We don't even have to like everyone around us, or be liked by everyone. But we must *respect the positions* our colleagues hold on

the team and work on building good working relationships. We must find common ground, and keep working
on earning trust though our own behaviors.

Like the frontline sales audience in Atlanta a couple of months
earlier, this audience, too, reacted positively. Once we were aligned
and committed, we focused on executing for results. I used the
same team-building approach at the other companies that I led.

To build trust around you, start with the right attitude. Care
about the people you work with. Catch them doing something positive. Interact with authenticity and with a smile. Lower your voice
when you feel you may be losing control. In this age of e-mail, send
a short handwritten compliment. It is amazing how much power
gets unleashed with a positive attitude.

*Aligning people around a shared dream becomes easier if you first
earn their trust.*

DRIVE THE VIRTUOUS SPIRAL UPWARD

At our first GLT meeting for PNU in March 1998 in Copenhagen,
one of our best and most credible country managers, Rod Unsworth,
was at the podium. Rod, who ran PNU Australia, explained how we
were finally starting to move from a downward spiral of declining
trust, declining alignment and declining market shares and profits to an upward spiral of increasing trust, increasing alignment,
improving execution and increasing profits (Figure 6.1).

At this GLT meeting, we constructed a graphic image of a virtuous spiral so that our PNU people could visualize the power
of earning trust and of alignment. We called it the *Executional
Excellence Spiral* (Figure 6.2). This became a fundamental part of
my Playbook.

In early 2003, when I became CEO of Schering-Plough, earning trust was a challenge. The company was bleeding cash; it had
recently agreed to pay a fine of half a billion dollars to the FDA and
it was the subject of criminal investigations.

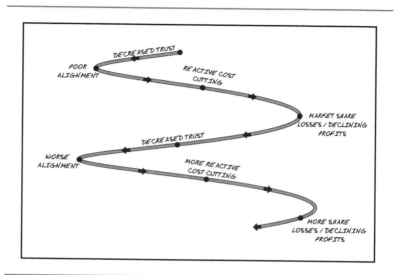

FIGURE 6.1   The Downward Spiral

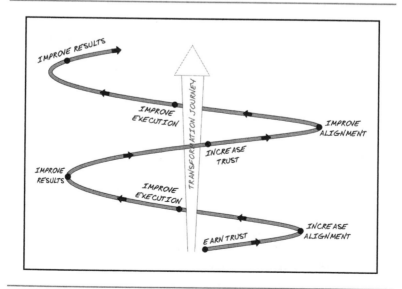

FIGURE 6.2   The Executional Excellence Spiral

Our starting point on trust and alignment was low. As Tony Butler, a well-known financial analyst, noted in September 2003, "Hassan did a nice job at Pharmacia, but this is a different bag of rocks to turn into diamonds."[1]

In October 2003, I attended a national sales meeting in Atlanta. At a pharmaceutical company, the sales force is a vital link in capturing the value generated in R&D. The 3,000 people present were not happy. Only a few weeks earlier, we had cut the dividend, frozen salaries and eliminated almost all bonuses, including my own incoming contractual bonus.[2] In addition, our blockbuster allergy drug, Claritin, lost its exclusivity and had not been replaced.

To make matters worse, we had announced a change in the salary/bonus split among the sales force from 60/40 to 80/20 as a way to inspire them to think of themselves more as medical information professionals than commission-driven sales reps. We were taking money out of many of their pockets, but we knew it had to be done. The old compensation structure was not building customer trust. Instead, it was creating a hard-sell environment in which many of our people chased today's commission-driven sale, and not tomorrow's long-term relationship.

Although I was getting credit for just showing up in Atlanta, the skepticism in the room was nevertheless palpable. I stood in front of our sales force and told them I needed their help. I said that there was one very important thing they could do for me, for the company and for themselves: "If you are put in a position where you must decide between making a sale that involves doing something you don't feel comfortable with—something you won't be proud of later—and walking away from that sale, then walk away. As your CEO, I'm telling you to choose long-term trust and integrity over short-term gain."

The audience had not expected me to say this, especially at a time of declining sales and profits. I was making a decision that I believed was right, even though it might be unpopular. Many stood

---

[1] John Simons, "Is It Too Late to Save Schering?" *Fortune*, September 15, 2003.

[2] My contractual bonus was estimated to be $2 million.

to lose even more bonus money by heeding my words, at least in the short term. Maybe some would think I was crazy. After a few quiet moments—during which time I thought the audience could go either way—they started to give me a standing ovation and kept applauding for a long time. The group was experiencing catharsis. *Yes, they wanted to do the right thing!* I was on my way to earning their trust.

That was a game-changer—one of several turning points for a company that many thought was on its last legs. Having won their trust, I focused on building alignment so we could improve execution and turn the downward spiral into an upward spiral. SGP employees sent notes and e-mails to my "Fred Hassan direct" mailbox from around the world about what they thought our new company should look like.

This input helped compose the core document. The SGP core document helped us establish what a high-performance culture would look like. We encouraged employees to make it their "say who we are, do what we say" covenant. Every member of our senior management team was expected to take it seriously and to personally model it. We required that the statement "Earn trust, every day" be printed on the back of everyone's business cards.

Appendix C: "Values Matter" outlines the values in the SGP core document that helped form the basis of our everyday expected attitudes and behaviors (See Appendices at back of the book). While some of these values appear to read as corporate speak, in a company of 50,000 people in 60 countries they greatly helped with building mutual expectations and interpersonal contracts.

In Chapter One, we discussed the power of humility. There is a certain amount of humility in the statement "Earning Trust." It means that one cannot assume trust, or demand it, or take trust for granted. Trust must be earned and re-earned every day. This shared sentiment helped us build extraordinary alignment. The office lights burned late into the dark winter evenings. People looked forward to coming to work on Monday morning. Voluntary turnover fell to record lows, even as star employees got targeted by other companies once news got out about SGP's transformation.

Probably my proudest moment, and the moment when I realized we really had transformed the company, was in March of 2007. I was the keynote speaker at the Council of Institutional Investors (CII) meeting in Washington, DC. CEOs are generally leery of this group, but I was warmly introduced by Damon Silvers, the associate general counsel for the AFL-CIO. I later overheard an important investor tell an SGP board member (who was there to meet investors), "This is an example of how passionate people can become aligned and create a high-performance machine out of thin air."

Equally gratifying was the alignment we built with the authorities, especially the FDA. In the past, this regulator had accused SGP of taking the public's trust for granted. I personally visited FDA officials, at levels ranging from the district level to the highest level at the center, on numerous occasions to share updates of our transformational journey, acknowledge the work that still needed to be done and ask for their advice. The FDA, in turn, started to publicly cite SGP as a company that "got it." In fact, the agency conveyed their newly developed trust by asking me to be an early commentator on their 2004 "Critical Path" document, aimed at helping safer, better drugs to reach patients faster and with less wasted costs for their R&D sponsors.

At all my companies, I worked hard to convince people that building trust and alignment is critical. This was especially important with the sales reps. When I was running Wyeth Pharmaceuticals in the early 1990s, I had an opportunity to accompany a sales rep on a field visit in Hudson County, New Jersey. As the rep was making his pitch, the doctor reached down into his drawer, took out an aerosol can marked "Bull****" and started spraying it at the rep. Some of the spray even came my way, even though I was only observing! On my way out, I counseled the shaken young man that it is better to earn trust with straight talk than to say things that are not credible. I know he learned a valuable lesson about trust that helped him become a better salesperson.

Trust takes a long time to build, takes a short time to lose and then takes a much longer time to rebuild—if it can ever be rebuilt at all. Without trust, there can be no real alignment and no excellence in execution.

Drive the virtuous spiral upward by building trust, building alignment and improving execution.

LINK STRATEGY WITH EXECUTION

Once competent and aligned people are working well as a team, they can effectively answer the questions "Where do we want to play?" and "How do we win?"

Once the strategy is set, the leader must keep it vibrant and execute for results. The following are the best ways to keep the strategy vibrant:

- Keep it simple. Get the buy-in.
- Regularly pressure-test the underlying assumptions. Make course corrections.
- Relentlessly link strategy to execution. Always remain hungrier than the competition. Hold yourself and the team accountable.

At SGP, we articulated our strategies around a six- to eight-year action agenda. To build credibility for the action agenda, we communicated it repeatedly using multiple platforms, and experienced early wins. Getting this buy-in with a workforce that, over the previous several years, had been made skeptical by frequent and reactive "initiatives" was a major achievement. In fact, I inherited "initiative fatigue" in all my new assignments, and it always took credible work to make people believe that this one was for real.

One important way to continue building trust and alignment is to work hard at overcoming the conventional divorce of strategy and execution, not only in terms of ownership and accountability but also in terms of transmission losses and time delays. At SGP we especially encouraged active interactions and cultural fusion between the "think its" and the "do its," as visualized below. The planners must be tightly linked to the implementers and vice versa.

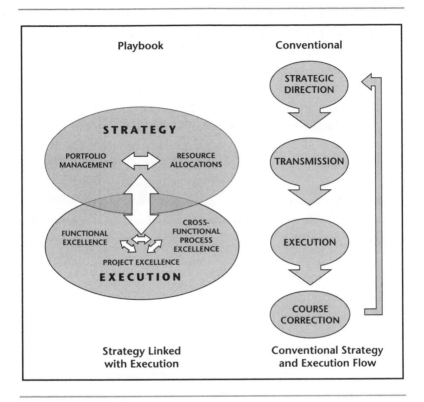

FIGURE 6.3   Link Strategy to Execution
Source: SGP/Merck

In many cases, they should be the same people. "Figure 6.3 shows this difference versus the conventional mechanisms."

Linking strategy to execution is key.

KEEP IT SIMPLE, KEEP IT STEADY

The Executional Excellence Spiral functions best in organizations that have simple and sturdy strategies that don't need to be changed much over the years. Many companies are pressed to launch new strategic initiatives as a way to create excitement at their scheduled events, such as analyst meetings. As time passes, their changing strategies start to look like a "flavor of the year" or "flavor of the quarter," and therefore begin to lack executional credibility. In contrast, sustained patience with a good strategic direction enables more executional traction and improved productivity.

Strategies are best articulated in a few straightforward sentences. They must become the centerpiece of a relentless communications effort aimed at all employees, but especially the frontline managers. When frontline managers can easily repeat the same strategy to *their* people, it becomes easier to make the rally cry "Execute, execute—day in, day out."

At SGP, we kept it simple and steady via a three-pronged strategic thrust:

1. Grow the top line.
2. Grow the pipeline.
3. Reduce costs and invest wisely.

During the six years that I was at the helm of SGP, the only change in these three was during a period when "contain costs" was substituted for "reduce costs."

Obviously there were brand strategies, R&D strategies, supply-chain strategies, IT strategies and country strategies, which supported the three-pronged strategic thrust. The basic strategies, however, became the unifying force for 50,000 employees.

Once the basic strategy is clear, then execution becomes everyone's strategy.

MAKE PRIORITIES, ALLOCATE RESOURCES

There is a military saying, "At the point of contact, apply the maximum force." Good leaders put their force toward a strategic opportunity or, for that matter, toward nipping an incipient problem in the bud. The best leaders are brutal with their resource allocation so that they can excel at what they do.

Wyeth's victory over Bristol-Myers in the Advil/Nuprin shoot-out in the mid-1980s is a classic example of this. Wyeth's product, Advil, came out at the same time as Nuprin in the newly created ibuprofen U.S. consumer market for pain relief. Advil benefited from the consumer unit president's personal attention, willingness to order supplies at risk, concentrated promotional spending up front and detailed pre-planning—down to having the trucks ready to ship the day after approval! Nuprin disappeared from the stores as Advil's spiral of success kicked in.[3]

In this digital age, the daily information flow is unrelenting. The Pareto principle, which states that for many events, roughly 80 percent of the effects come from 20 percent of the causes, is more relevant for priority setting and sequencing than ever before. The "critical few" need to be singled out for special attention, while the "maintenance many" need to get their maintenance share of resources. The "long tail" of less important products or projects or opportunities needs to be harvested, selectively maintained or divested depending on the circumstances.

In my Playbook, one method of prioritization and sequencing of activities is to roll out new products first in countries where one can put in maximum resources for maximum market share—and even market leadership.

Wyeth introduced the blockbuster Effexor (for depression) in this way during the 1990s. In spite of the crowded antidepressants market, Effexor went on to become a $4-billion annual sales product. The conventional "spread the dollars" approach, whereby individual country operations receive their pro-rata allocations of resources, invariably results in a few countries with high market shares and a few that are failures, with the majority settling for mediocre penetration.

In setting daily priorities, you can't allow the *urgent* to crowd out the *important*. For instance, even as we worked hard to stop

---

[3] Stan Barshay, the consumer unit president, went on to do important transformational work at the consumer unit of Schering-Plough with the allergy brand Claritin.

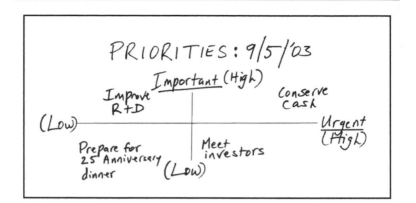

FIGURE 6.4   Both Urgent *and* Important Projects Need Attention

the bleeding during 2003–4 at SGP, we were also taking steps to improve our R&D—something that led to a tremendous upgrade in our late-stage R&D pipeline by 2008. Figure 6.4 is an illustrative example of where some of my fundamental priorities at SGP ended up on the chart. I discussed and shared this fundamental chart with my strategic advisers.

In this age of turbulence and information noise, our personal focus and concentration as senior leaders becomes even more important. We should be relentless in digging in. I try to check e-mail and return most phone calls only during the downtime between my "focus chunks" (usually 40 to 90 minutes), when I concentrate on the task at hand. We should chip away at the important tasks every day, while also dealing with the most urgent ones.

Good resource allocation includes good capital-allocation discipline. If capital is tied up for a long time in a low-producing asset, then the cost of capital has an unforgiving compounding effect on the internal rate of return on investment capital. At PNU and PHA, we divested more than a dozen significant operations because we wanted to invest in our core business, and also return money to the shareholders through share buybacks. Our attitude was that we were stewards for shareholders, and even if we liked these businesses, they had to go. In the private-equity environment I work in today, I have grown to realize that I could have taken an even sharper pen to capital allocation when I was running operating companies.

Tough calls on resource allocation allow the few driving strategies to become more visible for relentless follow-through.

MAKE THE STRATEGY EXECUTABLE

Since linking strategy to the Executional Excellence Spiral is a Playbook feature, and execution is 80 percent of success, I will share some more detail on how to make the strategy more executable.

Say It Again, Get the Buy-In

Repetition is a good thing in getting your various audiences— whether they are in the boardroom, the global town hall or on Wall Street—to buy into what you are doing. Repeating the same basic strategy in a few sentences builds not only clarity but also trust and alignment. A CEO's role as the "chief persuasion officer" is very important with the company employees, with the board, with external constituencies and especially with investors.

Repetition of strategy builds clarity, trust and alignment.

Regularly Pressure-Test the Underlying Assumptions, then Course-Correct

Regularly pressure-test the underlying assumptions upon which your strategy is based. Forced questioning to fight group politeness or groupthink is a good way to encourage candor. Forced questioning is related to encouraging deep drills on "why," "why not," "how," "what if" type questions to pressure-test the initial assumptions or the initial recommended strategy.

When I joined Sandoz in 1972, fixed five-year and ten-year plans were in vogue. I rapidly learned that a plan was only as good as the first encounter with new assumptions. The macros can change unpredictably. A competitor can show more cunning or more resolve than you had expected. An innovation project can create surprise on the upside (or downside). Or perhaps your original plans were not sufficiently pressure-tested. The key is to have a *strategic direction* that remains attuned to changing realities, but does not wander with every episode.

If the assumptions change, then make adjustments in the strategy and communicate those changes. The culture should facilitate *nimbly* seizing new opportunities as they open up, and playing effective defense when necessary. When the Monsanto opportunity arose in 1999, and the Organon opportunity in 2006/2007, not only did we seize the opportunities, but we also clearly communicated that these strategic game-changers were part of our already announced "beyond the turnaround" strategic direction.

Strategy is better converted to execution if it is regularly pressure-tested and appropriately course-corrected.

Relentlessly Execute, Remain Hungrier than the Competition, Hold Yourself and the Team Accountable

It is important to build into your organization's culture a bias to execute and a bias to remain hungry. Too many smart leaders are fuzzy with their expectations and accountabilities. People who have been trusted with execution must be held accountable.

If natural entropy is allowed to occur, companies and individuals become less motivated as they experience more and more success. Many organizations go from being hands-on start-ups to entrepreneurial growth companies. But, if they do not actively reinvent themselves, they can go on to become lumbering bureaucracies or even aristocracies. When this is allowed to happen, hungrier existing competitors or new competitive disrupters will eat away at the company's fundamental strengths. That's why strategic tuning in and reinvention is not only good offense, it is also good defense.

Making the strategy executable helps drive the Executional Excellence Spiral.

BUILD AN ATTITUDE OF URGENCY

I worked hard to embed urgency in my own life. In taking on tough challenges, I had to have this attitude. Having an attitude that drives you to find the most urgent problems—and then rapidly go after them—is probably the most important first step in starting a journey of transformation. *But urgency must be accompanied by sustainability.* For example, establishing a new headquarters in New Jersey was my "dive in headfirst" move after I took over as CEO of PNU in 1997. Once we consolidated the company's Kalamazoo, Stockholm and Milan locations into a new central headquarters, we were well on our way to putting our Playbook into action. Our Team at the Top came together quickly. We assembled A-players who were good at what they did, who also were good team players and role modelers, and then moved forward with innovation, speed and flexibility. To create a sense of what we called "new thinking, new capabilities, new urgency," we branded PNU as a $7-billion start-up.

Many in the business press like to write about new CEOs "cleaning house," but my Playbook is to be fair in assessing people because the people who remain from the previous management team often enrich the new team with their competence and their corporate memory.

At PNU, Göran Ando, the previous deputy CEO and head of R&D, was among those who had been seen as candidates for the CEO post that I now held. Many assumed that Göran would leave. I benchmarked him against the best R&D executives in the business and he made the cut by a large margin. I worked hard on building a relationship with him. Our mutual candor created trust, and he turned out to be not only a great R&D leader, but also a great executive team player and confidant on whom I could always count to speak his mind.[4] His "reconfirmation" as a member of the Team at the Top also sent an important message to other (Swedish) former Pharmacia executives, and they joined Göran in endorsing our strategy and executing it with a heightened sense of urgency.

Building an attitude of urgency helps secure repeated wins.

KEEP A COOL HEAD WHEN THE DISCOMFORT ZONE FINDS YOU

Things happen. When they do, companies are differentiated by how well they deal with a crisis or a sudden problem, and how well they recover. Role modeling by the CEO and the Team at the Top during a crisis is important in preventing fear, which reduces productivity. While swift and urgent action is often needed, it must be done with crisp discipline and a sense that "we are all in this together."

My team worked hard on developing processes to encourage news to travel fast. We always had a core team in each of the companies that I ran (Sandoz U.S., Wyeth Pharmaceuticals, PNU, PHA, SGP). These core teams, which were composed of seasoned executives who represented diverse disciplines, assessed and categorized events for importance and urgency. If the core team instructed that the event be put in the "important" or "urgent" category, then dedicated action teams that represented the affected functions would make it their priority to lend support. These systems carried acronyms, like EPAMS (Emergency Planning and Management System) at Sandoz, or PREP (Preparedness Response Process) at SGP. Since safety concerns would always be paramount, these core

---

[4] Göran's executive credentials enabled him to become CEO of a leading British biotech company following the PHA/PFE merger in April 2003. He will become chairman of Novo Nordisk, a $80-billion-plus-market-cap company, in spring of 2013.

teams were led by MDs (Dr. Göran Ando, head of R&D at PNU and PHA, and Dr. Robert Spiegel at SGP, for example).

The core teams were well prepared to not only manage the immediate issues, but also to deal with additional twenty-first-century challenges, such as 24/7 cable networks.

We are human. We are emotional. But, as CEOs, we have to keep a cool head and continue to show our commitment to our jobs, even when it gets hot. Just imagine the effect on the rest of the company if we start getting depressed or panicky.

Being prepared for and dealing with setbacks differentiates strong leaders from average managers.

POWER UP THE BOARD

In the twenty-first century, the role of boards has become even more important in overseeing management. Just as one of the most important personal decisions we make is who we marry, the most important decision a board makes is who it selects or reconfirms as CEO.

I give the boards of PNU and SGP credit for having had the courage to benchmark their incoming CEO selection decisions via an outside/inside look. When a CEO is already in the saddle, it remains the board's duty to cold-bloodedly assess that person, at least annually, to make sure the company has an effective leader at the helm. Boards must conduct frequent non-management executive sessions with enough time and lots of candor about the CEO, her strategy, her people choices and her role modeling.

Having had board experience at nine public companies, I have seen three CEO exit decisions. The following are some tough, simple questions to ask about a CEO:

- Is the CEO well grounded in reality, with a strategy that will develop traction?
- Is the CEO nurturing a team that can compete effectively against its best competitors?

- Is the CEO developing strong organizational health so that employees are encouraged to earn trust, to align and to give their best?
- If there was a benchmarking process today, would this CEO make the cut?

It is key to have quality board members and a board team that meshes well. The most important criteria for board-member selection are attitude, behavior, fit and judgment ability. I was fortunate to have strong, supportive, questioning boards at the three large public companies where I served as CEO.

At SGP we started in 2003 with a reputation that made some potentially good board members pass us up in favor of companies with "safer" reputations. Later, that situation changed and we attracted three very strong new board members.[5] Our board dynamics were unusually productive. There was a lot of courage and candor among SGP's board members in asking tough questions, requesting follow-ups, offering tough comments in a respectful manner and debating with ease. We tried hard to facilitate easy access for the board to our people other than me. At every meeting, I also insisted on a non-management executive session where I was absent, and usually with nothing else on the agenda afterward so that there would be no rush by Lead Director Pat Russo to end the session early. The CEO needs the opportunity to use the board as a value-adding team that goes well beyond the usual board task of voting on resolutions.

It helped that we had a first-class educational program for the board under the leadership of Susan Wolf, one of the best corporate secretaries in our class of S&P 100 companies. Our board members got to thoroughly know SGP's business, and were able to add extra value to the organization. The unusually innovative

---

[5] Craig Thompson, MD (currently head of Memorial Sloan-Kettering Cancer Center in New York), Bob Kidder (who became chairman of Chrysler at its difficult time in 2009) and Jack Stahl (former president of Coca-Cola and Revlon).

board-education program that Susan developed was highlighted in a professional publication on corporate governance in 2011.[6]

By immersing the board in the strategy, and using almost every board meeting to conduct a strategic conversation, we could move fast when events occurred. The reason we were able to move on Organon with such speed was because it had already been pre-identified as a good fit within our "Build the Base" strategy. So, when the window opened, we moved as one team, and were able to announce an agreement just before the Organon IPO road show was set to kick off.

SGP's board did a good job earning trust with important shareholder constituencies such as CalPERS, CalSTRS and the Council of Institutional Investors. These groups applauded, for instance, our proactive work on hearing from our shareholders on executive and board compensation. At a time when there was no legislated rule or even a "say on pay" proposal in the proxy vote among shareholders, the SGP board distributed a survey to its shareholders on the topic and posted the results on the SGP website. Those results were much more informative than a voting number that boards see after every annual meeting.

Shareholders start to put pressure on boards when a trust deficit builds up. The CEO has to keep filling his or her reservoir of trust, so that the trust holds when the downdrafts occur. I was fortunate that in my 12 years as a public-company CEO, my board did not have to defend me to the shareholders. Even during my initial dark days in 2003 at SGP, when two leading institutional investors wanted to show their anger, I was there right away in dialogue with them—explaining to them my action agenda that was aimed at fixing the company and asking for their help.

A high-EQ CEO fosters, appreciates and utilizes a strong and independent board.

---

[6] Susan E. Wolf et al., "The Case for Customized Board Education," *Corporate Governance Advisor* 19, no. 1 (January/February 2011): 1–7.

ONCE THE STRATEGY IS CLEAR, MAKE *EXECUTION* THE STRATEGY

Making strategies happen is the hardest part of being a CEO. *Leading the execution cascade is the CEO's job.* By working hard on aligning individual goals with the CEO's goals, we were able to unleash enormous executional productivity at all the organizations I led. We insisted on clear executional basics such as priorities, activities, responsibilities and deadlines. We also encouraged all individual action plans to have regularly monitored scorecards. Our operating discipline became a source of pride. As our better-than-expected results kicked in, we built even more trust, more buy-in, more alignment, even better execution and better results.

As mentioned earlier, I have developed over the years five strategic stepping-stones for transforming a sick company (or operation) and making it healthy. They are performed as an overlapping process, like a Gantt chart (Figure 6.5).

These steps are: 1) Stabilize, 2) Repair, 3) Turn Around, 4) Build the Base and 5) Break Out. Each of these five steps is described in

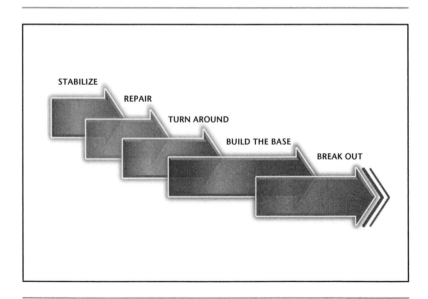

FIGURE 6.5   The Playbook Gantt Chart

Appendix F. This stepping-stone discipline helped keep our teams executing together and enjoying the journey.

Once the strategy is clear, make execution *the strategy.*

MULTIPLY THE POWER

The multiplier effect works to enhance productivity. Productivity can more than double if you improve *yourself* by 30 percent, then improve the effectiveness of the *people around you* by 30 percent, then get the *team* to improve its *collective* effectiveness by 30 percent (Figure 6.6). While the improvement percentage may vary, I saw this work again and again as I took on new challenges.

The multiplier effect can have a huge impact over a five-year horizon, as shown in the following hypothetical example.

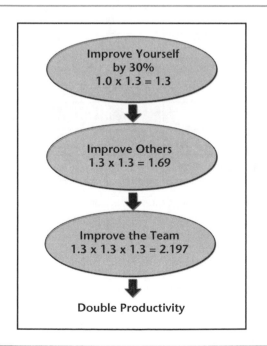

FIGURE 6.6 Multiply the Power

AMPLIFICATION OF RESULTS USING MY PLAYBOOK

Base Case

- Sales grow 3% per year.
- Profit after tax grows 5% per year.

Playbook Case

If productivity doubles via the multiplier effect:

- Sales now grow 6% per year.
- Profit after tax now grows 10% per year.

Over 5 years...

Sales

	Year 1	Year 6
Base Case	100	115.9
Playbook Case	100	133.8

Profit after Tax

	Year 1	Year 6
Base Case	100	127.6
Playbook Case	100	161.0

All growth percentages are expressed as compound annual growth rate (CAGR).

By multiplying the power and doubling the productivity, the profit growth index can more than double over a five-year period (refer to the above example) from a hypothetical +28% (base case) to +61% (Playbook case).

The multiplier effect magnifies the ABC Advantage.

Chapter Six Takeaway

Develop a winning upward spiral for the team by fostering trust and alignment and relentlessly building on the previous wins.

■ ■ ■

Chapters Four, Five and Six are about making the team stronger. These chapters build on the previous chapters which covered you becoming stronger and making the people around you stronger. Here, in summary, are the change-leadership takeaways from these three chapters.

Part Two	
Keep leading	**Pick good people.** **Align them.** **Motivate them.**
Role model your expectations	**Build trust.** **Expect winning behaviors.** **Expect leaders to lead.**
Keep winning	**Build trust and alignment.** **Execute for results.** **Drive the virtuous spiral.**

Conclusion What Keeps the Wheel Turning

CEOs and other leaders who succeed again and again share more than smart business acumen and drive. They build cultures where, by earning the trust of their people and improving alignment, they unleash a virtuous spiral of executional excellence that produces better results, which then build even more trust, more alignment, better execution and improved results—and the spiral continues upward.

It is worth reemphasizing that these productivity-enhancing cultures are, in my Playbook, a direct result of leveraging the ABC Advantage. Attitude, behavior and culture (ABC) are important because attitude stimulates behavior, which drives culture, which fosters the execution to secure success on a repeatable basis. Productive cultures not only enable effective strategies, executions and governance, but also provide the competitive edge in innovation.

When positive attitudes get reinforced, productive behaviors occur and cultures strengthen. Strong cultures not only enable operational or financial goals to be met but they also create personal satisfaction because people feel that they are contributing to a winning team effort. This personal satisfaction reinforces attitudes that then keep the wheel turning.

To become a senior leader, look at the leadership qualities mentioned in Part One of this book: qualities of character, heart, passion, curiosity, perseverance and courage. Look at the team-building ideas in Part Two. As a senior leader, make the case for change, include the ABC criteria in assembling a strong team, and then establish a vision and develop the mission, values, behaviors and operating principles. Make sure the Team at the Top buys in and becomes attitude carriers, behavior carriers and culture carriers. Boost morale by showing that team members are rolling up their sleeves and doing what they are saying.

Co-opt the frontline managers. Once the People part of the Power Triangle is in place, work on the Products and the Processes. Make ABC the *driving force* for each person on the team. Keep the strategy vibrant.

Expect all management teams to walk the talk with regard to the Leadership Quartet. Expect the Power Trident of Passion, Courage and Tenacity to become the norm and to create sustained individual and team energy. The team should then keep moving forward with purpose and unleash its Executional Excellence Spiral.[1] It should think long-term and visualize its transformational journey while securing its success markers along the way.

ABC always begins with attitude, attitude, attitude!

---

[1] Appendices A and B present some takeaways of this approach.

CHANGE-LEADERSHIP TAKEAWAYS

Make Yourself and the People Around You Stronger	
Be authentic	Value integrity, know who you are and know what you want to do with your life and career.
Be purposeful	Have clear goals, venture out and build energy and renew yourself periodically.
Be connected	Be connected with yourself, with people and with your environment.
Make the Team Stronger	
Keep leading	Pick good people, align them and motivate them.
Role model your expectations	Expect winning behaviors, expect leaders to lead and build trust.
Keep winning	Foster team alignment, execute for results and drive the virtuous spiral.

Afterword

I continue to have a lot of fun in my career. Fulfillment, to me, comes from my engagement and participation in improving leadership, culture, execution and results in the various organizations in which I am presently involved. My biggest joy comes from seeing valuable medical advances occur. Joy also comes from seeing people develop and do good things with their lives.

I keep hearing from colleagues all over the world that, even though they were not direct reports, they got to experience something during their period with me that helps them where they are now. *That feels good.*

In October 2012, I was chatting with David Cordani at a CEO conference. David, now entering his fifth year as CEO of Cigna, is dramatically changing the company from a classic U.S. financial insurer to a global health service company. David told me he remembers, when he was CFO and I was a board member at Cigna in 2003, that I had said, "one must reinvent every five years or so." That statement has become part of his thinking and he is now turning that philosophy into concrete action. *Those kind of positive stories also feel good.*

I have built a reputation of not shying away from challenges. I was recently asked to be the independent (non-executive) chairman of Avon, a company where I had been a board member. The company's challenges have been widely discussed in the media. I felt I had a duty to show up when I was needed. On October 5, 2012, the day the news came out that I would take this responsibility effective January 1, 2013, the Avon stock was up 7 percent for that day.

As a partner and managing director at Warburg Pincus, I see the global microcosm, whether it is different sectors (energy, information technology, media, industrial/consumer, financial services, health care and real estate) or geographies (United States, Europe, China, India, Brazil). I relish feeling the pulse of the changing global economy. Tuning in to social, political and demographic factors helps us gain strategic insights as we decide on investments in potentially new portfolio companies, or exits from certain portfolio companies that we own. It's fascinating to see how our firm's existing portfolio of about 130 companies ($30 billion under management) is performing and where we should be looking for new investments to replace our current positions in portfolio companies that may have matured under our watch. It is exciting to invest in earlier-stage companies with the hope that one of them may turn out to be our next hit or even mega-hit.

One job I particularly enjoy is looking for "backable CEOs" for our new ventures, or assessing and coaching the CEOs of our existing portfolio companies. One of my most satisfying experiences is being chairman of Bausch + Lomb (B+L), Warburg Pincus's largest equity investment in a portfolio company. It's a pleasure to see Brent Saunders, who joined me from Schering-Plough, as CEO do such a good job at changing the culture, enhancing execution and producing results. B+L was the first among three case studies cited by

IBM in its 2012 *Leading Through Connections* report. I was asked in August 2012, at the New York Stock Exchange amid a gathering of CEOs, to comment on B+L's turnaround. My Playbook, which Brent knows well and which he has deployed, has worked well again!

After Schering-Plough, I was pursued for a global public-company CEO job that had opened up shortly after the merger closed. Deploying my Playbook once again for *this* turnaround opportunity was tempting. This time, however, I was ready for yet another reinvention, and I decided to be more of an "investor" and less of an "operator." As with all my previous transitions, not a day of vacation separated me from my next assignment. It is fun to remain engaged!

So, why Warburg Pincus (WP) for me? This firm has an impressive pedigree and a good culture. WP pioneered private equity (PE) five decades ago and its latest fund (2008) of $15 billion is in the zone of the largest individual funds ever raised by PE companies. WP has a long and proud list of companies and people (including now-prominent entrepreneurs and CEOs) that it has helped to become successful in almost all the major geographies. What really drew me to WP was the importance it places on innovation and good management, its deep domain excellence in its sectors, its commitment to the long term, its respect for its people and its long-accomplished transition from founding personalities (who still dominate most other large private-equity companies).

I also elected to work with Warburg Pincus because humility and building trust are important values espoused by its co-presidents, Chip Kaye and Joe Landy. Also, working with the health-care team, led by its dynamic and inclusive leader, Bess Weatherman, is fun.

Yes, I continue to have a lot of fun!

Appendix A Serial Success— Playbook Summary

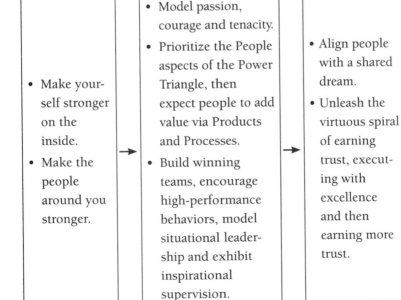

- Make your-self stronger on the inside.
- Make the people around you stronger.

→

- Model passion, courage and tenacity.
- Prioritize the People aspects of the Power Triangle, then expect people to add value via Products and Processes.
- Build winning teams, encourage high-performance behaviors, model situational leader-ship and exhibit inspirational supervision.

→

- Align people with a shared dream.
- Unleash the virtuous spiral of earning trust, execut-ing with excellence and then earning more trust.

Appendix B The Concepts Behind My Playbook

- Extraordinary and unexpected success can be achieved and repeated. Attitude, behavior and culture (ABC) are the common elements in serially successful CEOs.

- Success begins with reinventing oneself through self-awareness, self-development, self-control and self-drive.

- Success follows when one also reinvents one's environment— especially by building a good team and having the team move forward with a common sense of purpose.

- My Playbook includes the Diffusion Pyramid of Serial Success, which has three culture-enhancing pathways: the Power Trident, the Power Triangle and the Leadership Quartet.
  - The *Power Trident* comprises Passion, Courage and Tenacity among the people, and then translates these elements into the organization's innovation, speed and flexibility.
  - The *Power Triangle* is made up of People, Products and Processes. It always starts with People. Competent people, with the right attitudes, strong motivation and a clear sense of direction, will create a thriving culture that will develop good products and processes.
  - The *Leadership Quartet* consists of the four important winning leadership elements: the Winning Team Formula, High-Performance Behaviors, Situational Leadership and the Leadership Engine.
- By building a culture where people keep earning trust, aligning, executing and producing results, and then earning more trust, it creates a virtuous spiral called the Executional Excellence Spiral. This enables the organization to achieve extraordinary and sustained results on a repeatable basis.

Appendix C Values Matter

- **Business Integrity:** Do the right thing.

- **Candor:** Discuss issues in an open manner.

- **Courage:** Make the tough calls to manage ambiguity and to face adversity with quiet competence.

- **Emotional Intelligence:** Be in tune with yourself and with stakeholders and colleagues, and be sensitive to how your actions affect others.

- **Excellence:** Take pride in doing things exceptionally well.

- **Execution:** Get things done through a bias for action.

- **Faith:** Have faith in the company, in the products, in yourself and in your colleagues.

- **Humility:** Know what you don't know and know to ask for help. Share the credit.

- **Leadership:** Know the way, show the way and go the way. Others will follow.

- **Passion:** A driving conviction in what you are doing will generate energy.

- **Performance Recognition:** Differentiate by recognizing and rewarding those who contribute more.

- **Peripheral Vision:** See both the immediate task and the full picture.

- **Reach:** Develop your ability to see, and then act beyond the ordinary field of view and ambition.

- **Respect:** Recognize differences as assets and see the unique qualities of each person.

- **Teamwork:** Recognize that unity is strength, and directly work out differences.

- **Tenacity:** Stay the course and finish the job, even when unexpected obstacles develop.

- **Trustworthiness:** Earn trust through authenticity, dependability and sincerity.

Source: Adapted from the SGP core document

Appendix D　Bausch + Lomb's Rating System Descriptors

Consider performance against goals, high-performance behaviors and progress on development to determine the final rating. The relative importance of these factors may vary based on the employee's role and performance.

- **Leading Performance** (L): Delivered exemplary results while acting as a role model for high-performance behaviors; breakaway contribution with significant business impact this year, meriting special acknowledgment.

- **Strong Performance** (S): Delivered consistent performance at a high level; achieved solid results with strong business impact while demonstrating the high-performance behaviors required for success.

- **Proficient Performance** (P): Delivered sufficient results in all major areas with some business impact while generally demonstrating high-performance behaviors.

- **Developing Performance** (D): Delivered sufficient results in some areas but needs to be more consistent in all, including results and/or behaviors; must work to continuously improve performance.

- **Improvement Required Now** (I): Did not deliver results needed; significant shortfalls in high-performance behaviors; requires plan for significant improvement.

Source: Bausch + Lomb

Appendix E Guidelines for Expat Managers

- Begin with an attitude of respect for the local culture and demonstrate this respect by actively working to understand the country you are operating in.

- Listen and actively learn. Be open-minded. Avoid stereotyping the local situations, even if you have had negative experiences in the past.

- Be flexible on details, but stand firm on values and basic principles.

- Practice authoritative—not authoritarian—leadership. Build legitimacy.

- Use the company's global culture to build a strong local company culture. Use the operating principles from the company's core document to gain local traction.

- Build confidence and capability among local managers step by step.

- Play your own game. Don't get sidetracked if local competition cuts corners. Recognize that local business integrity standards among your competitors may be different than yours, and be prepared to be tested.

- Remember that second-tier local companies don't necessarily have the longer breath. Out-compete and outlast them.

- Cultivate relationships with the authorities at all levels, particularly before you need to reach out to them for a specific reason.

- Avoid taking sides among local political parties. People settle scores when they take power.

- Help other country operations on a peer-to-peer basis and ask for help from them as well. Encourage direct visits to learn and teach best practices.

Appendix F Stepping-Stones to Transformation

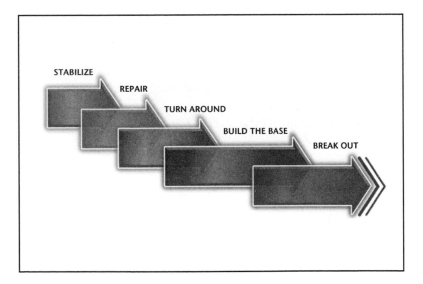

1. **Stabilize:** Show that you are in charge. Listen to and learn from customers, investors, opinion leaders and, above all, employees. Communicate the realities of the situation, then establish and

communicate the company's new vision, mission, values, high-performance behaviors and strategic direction. *Take early action steps that signal your downstream intentions.*

2. **Repair:** Take urgent actions that will address and correct issues from the past. Secure early wins to build credibility. Begin to upgrade and unify business units and functions. Strengthen dialogue with key stakeholders. Take urgent actions to protect the balance sheet. *Reach out to the frontline managers in order to create executional energy.*

3. **Turn Around:** Intensify executional excellence on three or four must-win action plans. Build team conviction and energy. Start the upward virtuous spiral of executional excellence. Start delivering sustained performance. *Fight the tendency to declare victory after a turnaround.*

4. **Build the Base:** Continue to build trust and alignment. Build breadth and depth of capabilities and continue to sharpen executional excellence. Leverage the new strength into new innovation, new country markets and outreach to new customer groups. Bring in new products via partnering, mergers and acquisitions or internal research.

5. **Break Out:** Keep communicating and celebrating wins in order to amplify organizational energy. *Leverage the strength that has been built.* Achieve continued superior performance and leadership that will carry the company through a major *step change* along its transformational journey.

Acknowledgments

I owe a lot to all my colleagues, bosses and partners who have enriched my life. It would not be possible to list all the names here.

Adam Snyder greatly helped me as my writing adviser, assisting me in arranging the contents of this book, in researching for facts and in distilling the early drafts. I am also grateful to Ken Banta and Kathy Bloomgarden for encouraging me to write this book, and to Bill Warden for help with fact validation, editing and input. Finally, I am very grateful to my staff, especially Debbie Noell who patiently soldiered through my markups in retyping my drafts.

I am grateful to my colleagues at Novartis, Merck, Pfizer and Bausch + Lomb for allowing me to mention case histories related to the operations they presently run.

I am grateful to all friends and relatives who have been my boosters. They gave me the self-confidence to keep going. I am especially grateful for the love and support from my daughters, Sabrina and Sarah, and my son, Daniel.

Any errors in this book are mine and are inadvertent, and a note of correction would be appreciated.

I thank all those who have recorded my business experiences and have granted permission to build on their work so others could benefit. I mention their work where appropriate with gratitude.

About the Author

Fred Hassan (New York) is a partner and managing director with the private equity firm Warburg Pincus. He is also chairman of Bausch + Lomb, as well as a board member of Time Warner and Avon, where he became non-executive chairman on January 1, 2013. Hassan is the former chairman of the board and chief executive officer of Schering-Plough Corporation. Prior to joining Schering-Plough in April 2003, Hassan was chairman and CEO of Pharmacia Corporation—a company that was formed in March 2000 as a result of the merger of Monsanto and Pharmacia & Upjohn. Hassan joined Pharmacia & Upjohn as CEO in 1997. Previously, Hassan was executive vice-president of Wyeth, formerly known as American Home Products, with responsibility for its pharmaceutical and medical products business. He was elected to Wyeth's board of directors in 1995. Earlier in his career, Hassan spent 17 years with Sandoz Pharmaceuticals (now Novartis) and headed its U.S. pharmaceuticals business.

Hassan received a BS in chemical engineering from the Imperial College of Science and Technology at the University of London, and an MBA from Harvard Business School. Hassan has chaired three significant pharmaceutical industry organizations: the Pharmaceutical Research and Manufacturers of America (PhRMA), the International Federation of Pharmaceutical Manufacturers & Associations (IFPMA) and the HealthCare Institute of New Jersey (HINJ). Hassan is also a member of The Business Council.

Index